Nairobi T

Guide 2024

A Traveler's Odyssey through Kenya's Dynamic Capital, Where Safari Meets Skyline, and Every Corner Tells a Tale

Robert D. Richmond

Copyright © Robert D. Richmond 2023

All rights reserved. No part of this publication may be reproduced, distributed, or transmitted in any form or by any means, including photocopying, recording, or other electronic or mechanical methods, without the prior written permission of the publisher, except in the case of brief quotations embodied in critical reviews and certain other noncommercial uses permitted by copyright law.

TABLE OF CONTENTS

MAP OF NAIROBI 7

INTRODUCTION 8

    Brief History of Nairobi 9

    Fun facts and FAQs 12

    Why Visit Nairobi 17

PLANNING YOUR TRIP 20

    Visa and Entry Requirements 20

    Best Time to visit 21

    Itinerary 23

    Tips to save money 26

GETTING TO NAIROBI 28

    How to Get There 28

ESSENTIAL INFORMATION 34

    Currency and Banking 34

    Language and Communication 35

    Local Customs and Etiquette 37

ACCOMMODATION 40

    Where to Stay 40

TOP ATTRACTIONS 58

Nairobi National Park 58

David Sheldrick Wildlife Trust 60

Giraffe Centre 62

Karen Blixen Museum 64

CULTURAL EXPERIENCES 68

Maasai Market 68

Kazuri Beads Women's Cooperative 69

Bomas of Kenya 71

TRANSPORTATION WITHIN THE CITY 74

Public Transportation 74

Car Rentals and Taxis 75

OUTDOOR ADVENTURES 78

Ngong Hills Hike 78

Karura Forest 80

Hot Air Balloon Safari 82

NIGHTLIFE 86

Trendy Bars and Clubs 86

Live Music Venues 87

Night Safaris 88

EVENTS AND FESTIVALS 92

Nairobi International Trade Fair 92

Blankets & Wine Festival 93

Maasai Mara Marathon 95

SHOPPING AND DINING 98

Unique Markets and Shops 98

Culinary Delights in Nairobi 100

Popular Restaurants and Cafés 102

DAY TRIPS FROM NAIROBI 106

Lake Naivasha 106

Amboseli National Park 108

Nairobi to Mombasa: A Coastal Adventure 110

PRACTICAL TIPS 114

Safety Precautions 114

Health Information 116

Useful Phrases 117

SUSTAINABLE TOURISM 120

Eco-Friendly Practices 120

Responsible Wildlife Tourism 122

Community Initiatives 124

CONCLUSION 126

MAP OF NAIROBI

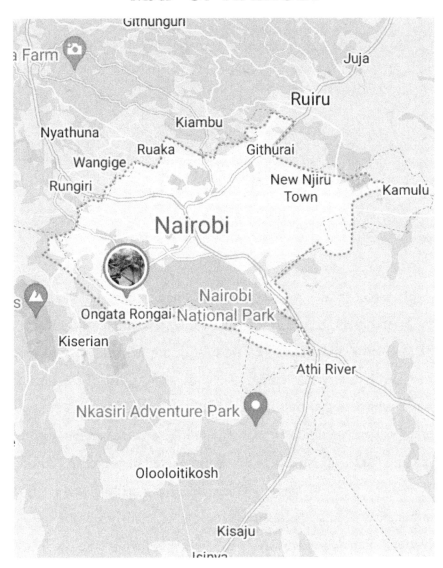

INTRODUCTION

A place that challenges preconceptions and sparks the imagination is located in the center of East Africa, where the pulsating rhythm of the metropolis meets the wild beat of the wilderness. Welcome to Nairobi, a city that embraces the dynamic spirit of the present while whispering secrets of its illustrious history. This is more than simply a travel guide; it's an invitation to discover the secrets, explore the terrain, and taste the undiscovered pleasures in Nairobi. When you turn the pages of this book, picture the acacia trees silhouetted against the deep reds of an African sunset. In Nairobi National Park, a refuge where the wild and the urban coexist in a delicate dance, feel the anticipation as the distant roars of animals resound across the park. Nairobi, however, is a tapestry woven with the strands of many cultures, rich traditions, and the unwavering spirit of growth, not only the sum of its famous scenery.

Underneath the surface is a city where tales are celebrated in the vivid colors of Maasai Market, whispered in the whispering leaves of Karura Forest and inscribed in every alley. Get ready to be mesmerized by the charms of the Giraffe Center, where gentle giants grace you with their presence, and the David Sheldrick Wildlife Trust, where abandoned elephants find refuge.

However, this guide is more than just a list of sights to see; it's a key to discovering Nairobi's nightlife's throbbing rhythm, hidden jewels, and local haunts. Every page invites you to immerse yourself in the spirit of a city that lives on contrasts, from the vibrant energy of its markets to the peace of its green areas.

Nairobi is an experience that must be discovered; it's more than simply a place to visit. So go out on this literary safari, wait for the excitement to develop, and be ready to be mesmerized by Nairobi's mysterious allure. Now is the start of your journey as we reveal the mysteries of this remarkable city below the equator.

Brief History of Nairobi

Kenya's vibrant metropolis, Nairobi, has roots that are deeply ingrained in the wild surroundings. Nairobi's history is a fascinating tale that takes readers from its modest beginnings as a railroad camp to its present-day position as a thriving city in the center of East Africa.

The story starts in the late 1800s when the British colonial authority set a camp at the Mile 327 marker to build the Uganda Railway. First meant to serve as a supply depot for the railroad construction, this camp quickly acquired the moniker "Nairobi," which comes from the Maasai expression "Enkare Nairobi," which translates to "cool water" and alludes to the Nairobi River that flows through the region. The early inhabitants did not know this temporary hamlet would develop into a bustling metropolis.

Its advantageous position along the railway line greatly influenced Nairobi's early expansion. The camp became a thriving community as workers and merchants arrived in search of possibilities. The recognized capital of British East Africa was Nairobi by 1907, which signaled the transfer of administrative authority from Mombasa to this expanding inland center.

The expansion of the metropolis was not without difficulties. Nairobi suffered economic losses and interruptions in the early 20th century due to the East African Campaign during World War I. Nonetheless, post-war restoration initiatives strengthened the city's resiliency and established the groundwork for further growth. Major social and political upheavals in the mid-20th century formed Nairobi's character. Nairobi became the epicenter of political agitation as the fight for freedom from British colonial control echoed through the streets. Important events in Kenyan history were seen in the city, such as the 1952 imposition of a state of emergency in response to the Mau Mau revolt.

Nairobi cemented its status as the capital of the newly established country of Kenya upon attaining independence in 1963. The city attracted individuals from many origins and nationalities by embracing its status as a political, economic, and cultural center. As skyscrapers started appearing across the skyline, Nairobi's transition into a modern metropolis increased.

Nairobi has become a major participant in innovation and technology worldwide in recent decades. The growth of innovation centers and companies in the area has given it the nickname "Silicon Savannah." This development shows Nairobi's capacity for adaptation and will to prosper in a world that is changing quickly.

Nairobi is more than simply a place; as we learn more about its past, it symbolizes the people who live here and their ability to adapt and persevere. Nairobi's history is a tapestry woven with the threads of victories, struggles, and the rich mosaic of its multicultural character, from its modest origins as a railway camp to the bustling metropolitan scene it is today. Discovering Nairobi is more than simply navigating its streets—it's a voyage through Time, a story that improves daily.

Fun facts and FAQs

Fun facts

1. Nairobi is often known as the "Green City in the Sun" because of its parks, gardens, and other green areas. The city's beautiful surroundings witness its dedication to preserving a balance between urban growth and the environment.

2. Elevation Hub: Rising to a height of around 1,795 meters (5,889 feet) above sea level, Nairobi is one of the world's highest capital cities. This height helps to maintain the city's moderate temperatures and pleasant environment.

3. Nairobi National Park is a unique city worldwide since it is the only one with a national park within its limits. Visitors may see various animals against the background of the city skyline in Nairobi National Park, just a short drive from the city center.

4. David Sheldrick Wildlife Trust: Located in Nairobi, this well-known elephant orphanage has substantially contributed to rehabilitating and conserving orphaned elephants. During the public feeding sessions, visitors may see gorgeous newborn elephants.

5. Giraffe Manor: Located in a boutique hotel where visitors may interact with and even feed resident Rothschild's giraffes, Giraffe Manor is one of Nairobi's most famous

attractions. Often poking their long heads through the windows, these gentle giants provide a unique and unforgettable experience.

6. Kibera, the Biggest Slum in Africa: Kibera, one of the biggest slums in Africa, is located in Nairobi. This statistic illustrates the socioeconomic variety of the city, even if it may not be very "fun" per se. The problems Kibera's citizen's experience are being addressed, and efforts are being made to make living circumstances better.

7. Maasai Market: This lively, colorful outdoor market provides a distinctive shopping experience. It is a must-visit location for travelers since it is ideal for purchasing traditional Maasai beading, antiquities, and other handcrafted products.

8. Nairobi is home to Karura Forest, an urban forest reserve with beautiful paths for bicycling and strolling. The magnificent Karura Waterfall in the forest brings a little peace to the bustling environment of the city.

9. Nairobi, the city in three counties, is situated at the meeting point of Nairobi County (home of the central business area), Kiambu County, and Kajiado County in Kenya. Nairobi's importance to the area is reflected in its unique geographic location.

10. Matatu Culture: The vivid, beautifully adorned minibusses known as matatus dominate the city's public transportation system. Every matatu is a moving piece of art that embodies the diversity and inventiveness of Nairobi's populace.

FAQS

1. **What makes Nairobi dubbed the "Green City in the Sun"?**

Nairobi's nice temperature and abundance of greenery have given it the moniker. The city is a revitalizing and energetic travel destination since it is filled with parks, gardens, and the famous Karura Forest.

2. **Is it accurate to say that Nairobi has a National Park within its boundaries?**

Of course! Visitors may have a safari experience without leaving the capital, thanks to Nairobi National Park, just a short drive from the city center. Numerous animals, including lions, giraffes, and rhinos, may be found there.

3. **What is the Nairobi Maasai Market's significance?**

The Maasai Market, which sells jewelry, handcrafted goods, and traditional Maasai clothing, is a cultural treasure trove for anyone looking for genuine Kenyan souvenirs and a lively cultural experience.

4. **Is it possible to engage with giraffes in Nairobi?**

You sure can! Visitors may get up close and personal with these gentle giants at the Giraffe Centre in Nairobi. A giraffe may be fed and even kissed, making it a special and unforgettable experience.

5. **Why is the "City in the Sun" nicknamed Nairobi so frequently?**

Nairobi has year-round sunshine and a temperate temperature. It's understandable why the city has attained this sunny distinction—it has more than 300 sunny days yearly.

6. **Does Nairobi provide any distinctive eating experiences?**

Of course! Nairobi has a vibrant and varied food scene. The city offers something for every taste, from trying Nyama Choma (grilled meat) in neighborhood spots to indulging in exotic cuisines at luxury restaurants.

7. **Can one have a hot air balloon safari in the vicinity of Nairobi?**

Yes, in fact! The unique chance to go on a hot air balloon safari above Nairobi's stunning scenery and fauna is available to visitors. This excursion infuses your Kenyan experience with a hint of enchantment.

8. **What does the Kazuri Beads Women's Cooperative stand for?**

"Small and beautiful" in Swahili, Kazuri Beads is a women's cooperative that creates one-of-a-kind, handmade clay beads. In

addition to helping out local makers, a visit to their studio provides insight into traditional workmanship.

9. **Could you inform me about any special Nairobi events?**

The annual Blankets & Wine Festival is a culture, music, and art festival held in Nairobi. Locals and guests gather for a fun celebration that features entertainment, delectable food, and a laid-back picnic vibe.

10. **Is Nairobi the center of efforts promoting sustainable tourism?**

Yes, in fact! Nairobi is aggressively working to promote eco-friendly travel. The city is dedicated to protecting its natural and cultural legacy, as seen by community-based projects and eco-friendly procedures at animal conservation facilities.

Why Visit Nairobi

Imagine yourself in Nairobi, the "Green City in the Sun," as the sun rises and warmly embraces the cityscape. There is a sense of excitement in this metropolis, where the opportunities are endless, like the savannah that extends beyond its boundaries. You could question, why go to Nairobi? Let me be your tour guide as you embark on this exploration.

Nairobi is, first and foremost, a city that defies classification. As you walk through its streets, you will be enthralled by the peaceful coexistence of the contemporary and the natural. Nairobi National Park invites you to see lions relaxing against the skyscrapers in a strange scene that perfectly captures the distinct appeal of the city. The park is a wilderness sanctuary within the city boundaries.

Nairobi is a cultural treasure trove. However, its appeal goes beyond safari travel. Imagine yourself perusing the Maasai Market, where vivid colors and elaborate crafts narrate the tales of a proud and long-standing past. Interact with the craftspeople, follow the beat of traditional music, and come away with souvenirs that embody Kenya in each stitch and bead.

Let's now discuss giraffes. You did read correctly. A wonderful encounter with these elegant animals may be had at the Giraffe Centre. Imagine feeding a giraffe with your hand while you are face-to-face and experiencing a connection that surpasses the typical barriers that separate people from animals. It's an encounter that permanently alters your perception of Nairobi.

But Nairobi offers much more than animals; its cuisine is a gastronomic journey that should not be missed. Your taste senses are in for a treat, from the posh restaurants serving a blend of world cuisines to the perfumed booths of local markets providing Nyama Choma, grilled pork specialties. Nairobi's culinary scene is as varied as the city, reflecting its cultural patchwork.

Here's a secret: Nairobi isn't simply a place to visit; it's a starting point for experiences that never compare. A bird's eye perspective of the country is provided by hot air balloon safaris, an incredible experience that deepens your appreciation of Kenya's natural beauty. Beneath you, the landscapes open out like a living painting, displaying vast plains and magnificent species in their native environment.

Nairobi's evening appeal emerges as the sun sets over this vibrant metropolis. Explore the exciting nightlife, which includes energetic bars, cultural events, and the catchy sounds of regional music that create a vibe that lasts well into the night. Under the stars, the metropolis that prospers during the day becomes an enthralling sight.

PLANNING YOUR TRIP

Visa and Entry Requirements

Visa Requirements

A visa is necessary for every traveler visiting Nairobi, Kenya. Visas for admission into Kenya are only available online. On the Kenya e-visa website, you may apply for a transit or single-entry visa.

Visa Application Requirements

- A passport with two blank pages is good for at least six months.
- Digital passport photo.
- Proof of yellow fever vaccination.
- Return or onward travel ticket.
- Proof of sufficient funds (USD 500 every 30 days of stay).

Visa Processing Time

Usually, visa applications are handled in three to five business days. It is advised to apply for your visa at least two weeks before your intended departure date.

Visa Cost

The cost of a single entry visa to Kenya is $51.

Entry Requirements

In addition to a valid visa, you will also need to present the following documents at the port of entry in Nairobi:

- Valid passport.
- Proof of yellow fever vaccination.
- Return or onward travel ticket.

Best Time to visit

January through February and June through September are the finest times to visit Nairobi during the dry seasons. The weather is pleasant, bright, and rainy throughout these months. This makes it perfect for outdoor pursuits, including hiking, game drives, and sightseeing.

Here is a more detailed breakdown of the different seasons in Nairobi:

- **January to February:** These are the hottest months of the year, with average temperatures ranging from 77°F (25°C) to 82°F (28°C). However, the weather is still pleasant, and there is little rainfall.
- **March to May** is the long rainy season, with heavy rainfall and thunderstorms. The roads may become muddy and treacherous, and some attractions can be blocked.
- **June to September** is the dry season and the best time to visit Nairobi. There is not much rain, and the weather is bright and warm.
- **October to December:** This is the short rainy season, with lighter rainfall than the long rainy season. However, the weather can be unpredictable, so it is best to be prepared for all conditions.

The Ideal Time to visit Nairobi to view animals is during the dry season. At this Time of year, animals tend to gather around water sources, facilitating their identification. During this period, millions of wildebeest, zebra, and gazelles traverse the Mara-Serengeti ecosystem as part of the Great Migration.

Itinerary

Day 1: Exploring Nairobi's Highlights

- *MORNING:* Fill up for a full day of adventure by starting your day with a delectable breakfast at Java House. Take a Nairobi Historical & Modernity Tour after breakfast to discover the lively culture and rich history of the city. See famous sites, including the Nairobi National Museum and the Kenyatta International Convention Center.

- *AFTERNOON:* Go to Tamarind Nairobi for lunch and savor some delicious seafood meals. See lions, giraffes, and zebras in their native environment by taking a half-day game drive in Nairobi National Park in the afternoon.

- *EVENING:* Savor a leisurely supper at The Talisman, a quaint eatery renowned for its delectable foreign cuisine. Explore the Karen Blixen Museum after supper to discover more about the life of the well-known Danish writer.

Day 2: Wildlife Encounters and Cultural Experiences

- *MORNING:* Get up close and personal with these magnificent creatures by visiting the Nairobi Elephant Orphanage and Giraffe Center to begin your day. After that, stop by Nyama Mama Delta Towers for a typical Kenyan meal.

- *AFTERNOON:* Learn about former street children's lives and inspirational tales by embarking on a Nairobi Storytelling Tour with Former Street Kids in the afternoon. Take in the local way of life while contributing to a worthy cause.
- *EVENING:* Carnivore Restaurant, renowned for its assortment of grilled meats, offers a distinctive supper experience. Go to Artcaffe for coffee and some delectable sweets after supper.

Day 3: Day Trip to Naivasha

- *MORNING:* Spend a day seeing the breathtaking Hell's Gate National Park and taking a boat ride on Lake Naivasha with a day tour from Nairobi. At Mama Oliech Restaurant, begin your day with a full breakfast.
- *AFTERNOON:* Take a trek or hire a bike to explore the stunning scenery after having a picnic lunch in the park. Remember to see some unusual species at the Crescent Island Game Park.
- *EVENING:* Travel back to Nairobi in the evening and dine at the Brazilian restaurant Fogo Gaucho Churrascaria, well-known for its mouthwatering grilled meats.

Day 4: Cultural Immersion and Shopping

- *MORNING:* Take a cultural tour of a Maasai community after visiting one to start your day. Discover the customs, culture, and way of life of the Maasai people. During the trip, have a traditional Maasai meal.
- *AFTERNOON:* Visit Nairobi's thriving marketplaces, such as the Maasai Market and the Kazuri Beads Factory, after the cultural tour. Purchase one-of-a-kind jewelry, souvenirs, and handcrafted crafts.
- *EVENING:* Savor the delights of genuine Ethiopian food over supper at Habesha Ethiopian Restaurant. Unwind at Zen Garden Restaurant with a cool drink after dinner.

Day 5: Nairobi National Park and Farewell

- *MORNING:* Explore Nairobi National Park, home to various animals, on your final day in Nairobi. Go on a self-drive safari or join a guided tour to see lions, rhinos, cheetahs, among other wildlife.
- *AFTERNOON:* Savor a picnic lunch in the park while admiring the amazing views of the skyline of the city. Visit the Sheldrick Wildlife Trust afterward to learn more about their work to save rhinos and elephants.
- *EVENING:* Tamambo Karen Blixen Coffee Garden, housed in the old home of renowned author Karen Blixen,

serves unforgettable farewell meals. Savor mouthwatering food from across the world in a lovely garden setting.

Tips to save money

Nairobi is a relatively affordable city, but there are still ways to save money on your trip. Here are a few tips:

- Dine at neighborhood eateries. Choose neighborhood eateries where Kenyans dine rather than tourist traps. You will spend a lot less for a cuisine that is at least as excellent as it gets.
- Use the transit system. The public transportation system in Nairobi is excellent and consists of buses, trains, and matatus, or minibusses. This is a much more affordable mode of transportation than a private driver or a taxi.
- Invest in a Nairobi Pass. With the Nairobi Pass, you may ride public transit for free and get unrestricted access to several popular sites in the city. If you want to see a lot of sights, this might be a terrific method to save costs.
- When shopping, haggle. In Nairobi, haggling is customary, so don't be hesitant to haggle over souvenirs and other items.
- Benefit from free events. In Nairobi, there are many free activities to do, including going to the National Museum of

Kenya, strolling around Central Park, or people-watching at one of the numerous marketplaces.

Here are some additional tips to save money in Nairobi:

- Remain at a guesthouse or hostel. A terrific way to meet other tourists is by staying in hostels or guesthouses, which are much less expensive than hotels.
- Prepare your food. One excellent method of cutting costs on food is to cook your meals. A lot of guesthouses and hostels allow visitors to use their kitchens.
- Steer clear of packaged water. The cost of bottled water may add up, particularly if you use it often. Refill your bottle at one of the numerous water dispensers around the city instead.
- Benefit from sales and discounts. Several Nairobi companies extend student, elder, and military discounts. Before making a purchase, be sure to inquire about any discounts.

GETTING TO NAIROBI

How to Get There

From Asia

There are many ways to get to Nairobi from Asia, depending on your budget, time constraints, and preferred mode of transportation. Here are a few options:

By plane: This is the fastest and most convenient way to travel from Asia to Nairobi. Many airlines offer direct flights to Nairobi from major Asian cities, such as Singapore, Hong Kong, Bangkok, and Dubai. Some popular airlines include:

- Ethiopian Airlines
- Kenya Airways
- Emirates
- Qatar Airways
- Turkish Airlines
- Singapore Airlines

Nairobi is often reached by plane from major Asian cities in 8–10 hours.

By bus: Although it is the least expensive alternative, using the bus takes the longest. Numerous bus companies provide direct bus service to Nairobi from major Asian cities, including Singapore, Bangkok, and Kuala Lumpur. It takes around four days and three nights to travel by bus from Bangkok to Nairobi and five days and four nights to go by bus from Singapore to Nairobi.

By train: While this is a more picturesque route, it is also more costly and slower than the bus. Although there isn't a train that goes directly from Asia to Nairobi, you may take one to Addis Ababa, Ethiopia, and then change to a bus to Nairobi. The train journey takes around three days and two nights from Bangkok to Addis Ababa.

By car: This is the most cost-effective and time-efficient alternative but also the most flexible. You may need to pass many countries if you travel from Asia to Nairobi, so be careful to research the visa criteria and get the required documentation beforehand. Driving Time from Bangkok to Nairobi is around ten days.

From South America

Depending on your budget and time constraints, there are a few different ways to get to Nairobi from South America.

By plane: This is the fastest and most convenient way to travel between the two continents. Several different airlines offer flights from major South American cities to Nairobi, including:
- Kenya Airways
- Ethiopian Airlines
- South African Airways
- Qatar Airways

- Emirates

Depending on your routing, flights from South America to Nairobi typically take around 15-20 hours.

By bus: This is the cheapest way to get to Nairobi from South America but also the most time-consuming. Several different bus companies offer services from major South American cities to Nairobi, including:

- Cruz del Sur
- Expreso Internacional Ormeño
- Andesmar
- Copacabana

Bus travel from South America to Nairobi usually takes three to four days, depending on your route.

By car: This is the most costly, but also the most daring, method to travel from South America to Nairobi. Should you want to drive, you will need a visa for every nation you enter and exit. You should also know the possible risks of driving in South America, including poor road conditions and criminal activity.

Depending on your route, the trip from South America to Nairobi usually takes two to three weeks.

From North America

There are several ways to get to Nairobi from North America: by plane, train, or bus. Nairobi is the capital city of Kenya and a major hub for transportation in East Africa. The options available to you will depend on your budget and preferences.

The plane is the fastest mode of transportation to Nairobi from North America, with flight times typically ranging from 14 to 16 hours. Several airlines offer direct flights from major cities in North America to Nairobi's Jomo Kenyatta International Airport (NBO), including:

- Delta Air Lines (from New York-JFK and Atlanta)
- Kenya Airways (from New York-JFK, Washington, D.C.-Dulles, and Los Angeles)
- United Airlines (from New York-JFK, Newark, and Washington, D.C.-Dulles)

You can also find indirect flights to Nairobi from most major cities in North America, with airlines such as:

- Air Canada
- British Airways
- Ethiopian Airlines
- KLM Royal Dutch Airlines
- Lufthansa

You may take a bus or a cab from NBO to your destination in Nairobi.

Traveling by train is more affordable than flying, but it takes longer. Although there isn't a train that goes directly from North America to Nairobi, you can ride one to either New York City or

Montreal, from which you can get an aircraft to Nairobi. Usually, the whole trip takes between 24 and 36 hours.

The slowest and least expensive way from North America to Nairobi is via bus. Though you can take a bus to New York City or Montreal and then change to a flight to Nairobi, there isn't a direct bus route from North America to Nairobi. Usually, the whole trip takes between 36 and 72 hours.

Flying is the easiest and quickest method to travel from North America to Nairobi. On a tight budget, you may consider traveling by bus or rail, but be ready for a longer trip.

From Europe

The quickest and most convenient way to get to Nairobi from Europe is by plane. Several airlines offer direct flights from major European cities, including:

- Kenya Airways (from Amsterdam, Frankfurt, and Paris)
- Air France (from Paris)
- KLM (from Amsterdam)
- Lufthansa (from Frankfurt and Munich)
- Swiss (from Zurich)
- Turkish Airlines (from Istanbul)

Flight times vary depending on your departure city, but most flights take between 7 and 8 hours.

If you are on a budget, you may consider flying into one of Nairobi's nearby airports, such as Jomo Kenyatta International

Airport (NBO) or Wilson Airport (WIL). Several budget airlines fly to these airports from Europe, including:

- Flydubai (from Dubai)
- RwandAir (from Kigali)
- Ethiopian Airlines (from Addis Ababa)

Although the flight durations to these airports are often longer than those to Jomo Kenyatta International Airport, the cost savings may be substantial.

Train travel is an additional means of transportation from Europe to Nairobi. London and Nairobi are connected by direct rail, and the journey takes around 14 hours. Before arriving in Kenya, the train passes via France, Belgium, Germany, Switzerland, and Austria.

If you are taking the train, you must first take an aircraft into London. Numerous airlines provide direct flights from major European cities to London.

Once in Nairobi, there are three ways to move about the city: bus, taxi, and matatu (shared minivan). Nairobi is also connected to several other Kenyan cities via train.

ESSENTIAL INFORMATION
Currency and Banking

The official currency of Kenya is the Kenyan shilling (KES). Banks, currency exchange offices, and hotels all allow you to swap your cash into KES. You will get a better exchange rate if you exchange your money before you depart.

Although credit cards are often accepted in Nairobi, it's a good idea to have extra cash with you in case of an unexpected expense. ATMs allow you to take out cash using a credit or debit card. However, be advised that ATM withdrawals in Kenya are subject to fees from Kenyan banks.

Here are some tips for using credit cards and ATMs in Nairobi:

- Make credit card purchases from reliable companies. There is a chance of fraud when using your credit card with street sellers or tiny companies, so proceed cautiously.
- Give your bank advance notice of your trip. By doing this, you may lessen the chance that using your credit card in Kenya will block it.
- Recognize ATM surcharges. ATM withdrawals are subject to fees at Kenyan banks. Before making any withdrawals, be sure to review the cost.
- Use your credit card to make hotel and travel reservations. Since using your credit card often entitles you to points and

discounts, this is a terrific way to save money on your vacation.

Here are some additional tips for managing your money in Nairobi:

- Make a thorough budget. Make a budget and keep track of your expenses before your trip. This will assist you in staying on budget and preventing overpaying.
- Safeguard your finances. If you bring a lot of cash with you, use caution. Whenever feasible, use your ATM or credit card instead.
- Recognize con artists. Nairobi is rife with con artists, particularly in the tourist districts. Give money to strangers with caution, and don't accept assistance from strangers.

Language and Communication

The official language of Kenya is English, but Swahili is the national language and is widely spoken by most Kenyans. Other languages spoken in Kenya include Kikuyu, Luo, Luhya, and Kamba.

English is widely used in Nairobi, especially in business, government, and education.

However, it is helpful to know a few basic Swahili phrases, such as:

- Jambo: Hello

- Habari: How are you?
- Nzuri: Good
- Asante: Thank you.
- Karibu: You're welcome
- Tafadhali: Please
- Hapana: No
- Ndio: Yes
- Saidia: Help
- Samahani: Sorry

Even if you don't speak Swahili or English well, you can still get along with people in Nairobi. In addition to being eager to assist visitors, many Kenyans also try to speak English or other languages.

Here are some tips for communicating in Nairobi:

- Be considerate and courteous. In general, Kenyans are very hospitable and nice. It is crucial to communicate with them in a kind and respectful manner.
- Talk clearly and slowly. Kenyans will comprehend you better as a result of this.
- Simplify your language. Don't use jargon or complicated language.
- Have patience. Communicating with Kenyans might take time, particularly if they don't speak Swahili or English well.

Local Customs and Etiquette

Nairobi is a multicultural metropolis home to a varied populace. However, there are still some local customs and etiquette that visitors should be aware of.

Here are some tips for following local customs and etiquette in Nairobi:

- Dress humbly. Since most Kenyans are conservative, it's crucial to wear modest clothing, particularly while visiting rural regions. Don't dress provocatively or wear short skirts.
- Shake hands when you greet someone. In Nairobi, it's traditional to shake hands while welcoming someone. Additionally, you could wish to greet someone with a "Jambo" (Swahili meaning "hello").
- Honor those who are older. In Kenyan culture, elders are held with great regard. It is traditional to address elders by their title and last name. For example, you might say "Mr. Smith" rather than "John."
- Don't use your left hand. In Kenyan culture, the left hand is seen as impure. Do not pass things, dine, or shake hands with your left hand.
- Think twice before speaking in public. Although most Kenyans are kind and inviting, they also keep to

themselves. Steer clear of touchy subjects like politics and religion while conversing in public.
- Be ready to negotiate. Nairobi is a city where haggling is frequent, particularly in marketplaces and souvenir stores. Never be scared to haggle for a better deal.
- Have patience. In Nairobi, things don't always happen when they should. Enjoy the experience and exercise patience and understanding.

Here are some additional tips for respecting local culture and customs in Nairobi:

- Respectfully visit places of worship. When attending a mosque, church, or any other place of worship, dress correctly and conduct yourself with decency.
- Consider the volume you're making. In general, Kenyans cherish stillness. Steer clear of loud sounds, particularly in public areas.
- Show consideration for the surroundings. Avoid littering and environmental pollution.
- Encourage regional companies. Try to support small, neighborhood stores when you shop in Nairobi rather than large, international chains.

ACCOMMODATION
Where to Stay

The Social House Nairobi, a Preferred Lifestyle Hotel

- **Location: 154 James Gichuru Road, Nairobi 00100, Kenya**
- **Hotel class: 4-star Hotel**

Imagine this: There are eighty-three bedrooms, each a cozy haven ready to envelop you in its allure. There are no generic rooms here; you'll encounter surprising areas that challenge norms. The insides? They are an unconventional tapestry, a symphony of hues and textures that move in unison with one another. Get ready for wonderful surprises at every corner.

Let's now discuss the gathering areas, which are the focal point of this unusual residence. Seven of them are arranged both inside and outdoors, beckoning you to escape the routine of everyday meetings. These spaces are more than simply meeting rooms; they are blank canvases for artistic expression and places to create lasting relationships.

Do you want more? Four eateries and pubs here promise a gastronomic adventure and a meal. Unique culinary traditions entice us, with every dish as a ticket to unexplored culinary realms. There are many culinary surprises, and each mouthful has its unique tale to tell as you relish the surprising tastes.

Then there is the leisure center, which consists of an outdoor pool sparkling in the African sun, a peaceful backyard garden whispering stories, and a gym calling out to the fit and active. As varied as the experiences you'll have within these walls are your alternatives.

The people, however, are the key component that sets this residence apart. Uncommon individuals, just like you, are looking for a place to belong rather than merely relax. The staff members here are more than simply employees; they are storytellers who spin tales of consolation and tenderness to evoke the feeling of an old friend coming home.

As the sun sets, be prepared for anything unforeseen. Things that don't always go as planned, nights that promise something unexpected. This home welcomes the unconventional; here, strange encounters result in life-long memories, and unusual décor serves as the setting for your unique adventure.

Movenpick Hotel & Residences Nairobi

- **Location: Mkungu Close, Westlands, Nairobi 49719 Kenya**
- **Hotel class: 5-star Hotel**

Discover the Mövenpick Hotel & Residences, a hidden treasure in the center of Nairobi, as the golden sunsets cast colors of rose and amber over the expansive metropolis. Imagine an African tapestry woven with colorful indigenous design, the warmth of welcome, and the appeal of expansive vistas that seem to go on forever.

The Mövenpick Hotel & Residences Nairobi, perched magnificently in the perennially popular Westlands area, is a tribute to the allure of the city's multiculturalism. It's a canvas on which your Nairobi trip is painted, not simply a place to lay your head.

A positive vibe that matches the city's beat greets you when you enter the foyer, decorated with details honoring Kenya's rich cultural past. The African design features are more than just ornaments; they are hints of a tale that entices you to become lost in the regional fabric.

Look forward to the unique characteristics that set Mövenpick apart as you go upstairs to your overnight residence. Every house, suite, and room is a haven of luxury and comfort. The roomy apartments provide a respite from the busy activity of the city, enabling you to relax and rejuvenate in an environment that skillfully combines luxury with the genuine beauty of Africa.

Let's now discuss the opinions—oh, the perspectives! Imagine waking up to the stunning Nairobi skyline, which reaches far into the distance. Beneath you, the city spreads out into a vivid kaleidoscope of colors and energy. The view from Mövenpick serves as a continual reminder that you are in the center of Kenya's capital, whether here on business or for pleasure.

The vibrant neighborhood of Westlands is another that begs you to explore. You are in a great position to explore the wide range of eateries, retail establishments, and cultural hubs that characterize this area from Mövenpick. Step out into the bustling streets and feel the city's pulse, knowing that your Mövenpick refuge of peace awaits you when you return.

Savor the gastronomic treats that Mövenpick has to offer as the day goes on. Savor a gastronomic symphony at the on-site restaurants, where regional and global cuisines combine to create a delectable experience. Every mouthful is an adventure, a synthesis of flavors that reflects the variety of Nairobi.

Radisson Blu Hotel, Nairobi Upper Hill

- **Location: Elgon Road Upper Hill, Nairobi 00100 Kenya**
- **Hotel class: 5-star Hotel**

Imagine a location where the African bush's wild energy meets the metropolis's throbbing pulse. Situated in the center of the Upper Hill commercial sector, the Radisson Blu Hotel is a five-star sanctuary that is just a short 20-minute drive from the airport and Nairobi National Park. It is more than just a hotel; it's a starting point for an incredible fusion of corporate sophistication with the romance of a Kenyan safari.

The Radisson Blu Hotel is tucked away in the heart of this vibrant city, waiting for you to explore everything it offers. Nairobi National Park, a world-class wildlife sanctuary, extends your journey with opportunities to see giraffes, wildebeests, and herds of zebras. The prospect of two exciting adventures—a prosperous business trip and an engaging Kenyan safari—unfolds as soon as you enter the foyer.

Our 271 opulent guestrooms and suites are proof of our commitment to providing maximum comfort. Every area is peaceful, with the alluring background of Nairobi National Park or expansive city vistas. You can easily connect to the outside world with the free Wi-Fi, and your every need will be satisfied with the fully stocked minibar. Our lodgings are irresistible not just because of their generosity but also because of the indisputable value they provide, which elevates each moment to the spectacular.

Our decadent breakfast buffet will tantalize your senses with a symphony of hot and cold treats, freshly baked products, and the fragrances of our egg and pancake station. The iconic "Morning Mary" becomes the catalyst that gets you through the rest of the day. It's a celebration as much as a meal and a fantastic way to begin your Nairobi experience.

Enjoy traditional world fare and Kenyan cuisine at the Larder restaurant as the day progresses, or take your dining game to the next level at Chophouse, our exclusive dining oasis. After a long day of meetings or exploring the local fauna, the Humidor Bar & Lounge beckons with its delicious appetizers and the ideal bottle of wine.

Invigorate yourself in our state-of-the-art gym as you tone your body in the city's background noise. Then, give yourself up to the tranquility of our spa—a haven where tension melts and renewal takes center stage. Our swimming pool is a visual treat, a peaceful haven in the middle of the bustling metropolis, where you can cool down with a refreshing swim or just soak up the warm African sun. However, our welcoming, amiable, competent staff makes the Radisson Blu Hotel stand out. Imagine being treated like royalty, with each encounter becoming an unforgettable and significant part of your travels. Our dedication to your safety is unshakeable. Our recent award of the highest accolade in the business, the Safehotel Certification, Executive Level, guarantees your peace of mind while in our care.

ibis Styles Hotel Westlands Nairobi

- **Location: Rhapta Road, Nairobi 00800, Kenya**
- **Hotel class: 3-star Hotel**

Imagine this: Global industry giants come together at the Westlands business area, a crossroads of innovation and trade. This vibrant neighborhood has become a booming hub of economic vitality due to the several global companies that have picked it as their headquarters. In the middle of this vibrant activity, our Hotel stands out as the perfect retreat for travelers looking for more than simply lodging—a comfortable, stylish, and convenient experience.

Every room in our house has been thoughtfully designed to entice you with bold colors, chic decorations, and a dash of trendiness as soon as you walk in. Our rooms are designed to cater to the requirements of contemporary explorers, providing a haven for rest and inspiration.

Our proximity to Jomo Kenyatta International Airport is a convenient beacon for travelers worldwide. We're just 20 kilometers away, and you can easily get there with our smooth transfer services or a few taps on your preferred taxi app. Let the city open out before you and forget about your travel concerns.

Situated in a prime location only 5 kilometers from the CBD of Nairobi, we provide a break from the bustle of the city while keeping you linked to its vital core. High-speed Wi-Fi guarantees that you will stay smoothly linked to the outside world even while you relax. It is more than just a promise.

Let's discuss business now. Our facilities, which include conference rooms that can hold up to 182 attendees, are designed specifically for the discriminating professional. We provide the framework for your success for every kind of event, from conferences to business get-togethers, ensuring that each one is successful and unforgettable.

However, life isn't all work and no pleasure. We have more to offer than just a boardroom. A fully furnished exercise facility awaits anyone looking for a refreshing workout. Our ground floor's modern casual dining restaurant and coffee shop beckons as the day draws closer. It's a gastronomic adventure for your taste senses.

Reach the summit to find our rooftop retreat, which provides 360-degree views of the Nairobi city. The sky is painted orange and gold by the unfolding sundowners against the symphony of city lights. Our recently built Stylish Restaurant welcomes you to indulge in a feast for the senses if you're craving something different.

Do not worry if you travel to the well-known Maasai Mara; we have carefully chosen activities to satisfy your desire. We have a Tours & Travel department prepared to take you on trips to the David Sheldrick Elephant Orphanage and Nairobi National Park. Take in the beauty of nature, see the giraffes' elegance, and walk the same pathways that the film "Out of Africa" chronicles.

Crowne Plaza Nairobi Airport

- **Location: First Freight Lane Jomo Kenyatta International Airport, Nairobi 00100 Kenya**
- **Hotel class: 4-star Hotel**

Imagine arriving at the Crowne Plaza Nairobi Airport feeling as comfortable and welcoming as you would walking through the colorful streets of Nairobi. It's an oasis where your travel stories find a home, not simply a hotel. Permit me to tell you the tale of this amazing four-star sanctuary.

The Crowne Plaza Nairobi Airport shows the city's dedication to quality. A distinct feeling of luxury is in the air as soon as you walk into the lobby. A sanctuary of peace, the rooms and suites entice tired travelers with promises of luxurious luxury and contemporary elegance. Lean back on the luxurious bed linens and let the soft murmur of the metropolis outside fade into the distance.

At the Crowne Plaza Nairobi Airport, your gastronomic voyage is an international study of sensations. You are cordially invited to enjoy a symphony of culinary pleasures at the on-site restaurant. Every mouthful is an occasion to celebrate, ranging from exquisite regional food to well-prepared worldwide cuisines. Imagine yourself enjoying fine dining under the Nairobi sky, with the city lights illuminating your surroundings while reliving the gastronomic creation.

The outdoor pool turns into your little aquatic sanctuary in the middle of the city. Imagine enjoying a nice drink, sipping on a delicious beverage, and enjoying the Kenyan sun. It is more than simply a swimming pool; it is a haven in the middle of the busy metropolis, a shimmering fantasy.

The gym is a body and spirit sanctuary for individuals seeking a refreshing break. Contemporary apparatus is prepared to accompany you on your journey towards well-being. Experience the vibrancy of Nairobi infuse every step you take as you work up a sweat.

Modern business facilities are available at the Crowne Plaza Nairobi Airport for the daring business traveler. Here, efficiency and style combine to create a successful atmosphere. The amenities are designed to meet all your needs, so your work projects will naturally flow with the luxury of your surroundings.

In an era when being connected is essential, the Crowne Plaza Nairobi Airport is a shining example of smooth connectivity. The whole area is covered with free Wi-Fi, so you can instantly share your Nairobi activities with everyone. Your adventure is extended into the digital sphere, seamlessly blending in with real-world events.

Villa Rosa Kempinski Nairobi

- **Location: Chiromo Road, Nairobi 00800, Kenya**
- **Hotel class: 5-star Hotel**

You enter Villa Rosa Kempinski and find yourself in a world where every little element has been meticulously chosen. The tastefully decorated hotel rooms entice tired visitors with the promise of comfort. Picture relaxing nights under the cool comfort of an air-conditioned room, watching your preferred TV programs on a stylish flat-screen, and enjoying a minibar that fits your preferences.

Let's now discuss the connection. In an era when keeping connected is essential rather than merely a luxury, Villa Rosa Kempinski makes sure you can move fluidly between discovery and the digital world. Free Wi-Fi is a liberating gift that lets you share your adventures in Nairobi with friends and family or plan your future trip from the comfort of your Hotel.

Nevertheless, Villa Rosa Kempinski's charm goes beyond your area. Imagine yourself standing on the rooftop patio, where expansive vistas of Nairobi seem to be a blank canvas. The city's pulse can be felt here, under the open sky, as the streets below resound with its heartbeat.

Villa Rosa Kempinski's hospitality goes beyond appearances; it's a dedication to improving your stay. A committed concierge is on hand to make your wishes come true and guarantee that every second is customized to your tastes. Room service transforms into a lavish symphony that delivers Nairobi's delights to your door.

As you enter a gastronomic paradise, Villa Rosa Kempinski greets you with open arms and a welcoming kitchen. A lavish breakfast that is a tasteful blend of regional and foreign cuisine sets the stage for your day of discovery. After exploring Nairobi's colorful streets all day, unwind with a cool swim in the pool—a peaceful time among the bustle of the city.

Located close to well-known sites like the Jamia Mosque and the Shri Swaminarayan Mandir, Villa Rosa Kempinski is a tactical haven for your trip to Nairobi. The Hotel's position offers an entry point to the best of Nairobi, whether you are a foodie or a seeker of cultural diversity.

In the neighborhood, there are places like Artcaffe and Artcaffe for delicious schnitzel for people with a flair for culinary explorations. Fans of seafood may sample the cuisine at Pizza Corner Cafe & Grill, Tatu Restaurant, and the charming Japanese izakaya Cheka.

Only a short walk away, the Nairobi Arboretum beckons with its rich foliage when the need to reconnect with nature strikes—a peaceful haven inside the city's embrace.

Radisson Blu Hotel & Residence, Nairobi Arboretum

- **Location: Arboretum Park Lane, Nairobi 00100, Kenya**
- **Hotel class: 4-star Hotel**

Welcome to a realm where the bustle of the city disappears and Time seems to stand still. This vast woodland reserve, tucked up next to Nairobi Arboretum, beckons with the prospect of exploration. It's more than simply a bunch of trees; it's an arboreal paradise, a haven for more than 300 rare tree species that tower above us as defenders of our natural history.

The Nursery's botanical tapestry is revealed as you walk along the meandering walkways; each tree represents a chapter in the tale of biodiversity. Giants with branches covered in a rainbow of leaves are straining for the sky. The native trees provide a pleasing harmony of hues and textures alongside foreign visitors, their roots firmly planted in Kenyan soil.

However, the Nairobi Arboretum's charm goes beyond its magnificent trees. It is a refuge for more than 100 bird species and a shelter for avian marvels. Just picture the delight of discovering a colorful avian orchestra, with every bird contributing to the organic melody. Your senses are delighted by the African Pied Wagtail's harmonious trill, the Speckled Mousebird's rhythmic pounding, and the White-cheeked Turaco's jovial chatting.

The Nursery provides more than simply a walk amid the trees for those who like exploring. A picnic or quiet reflection may be enjoyed on the secluded seats under the lush cover. You may encounter magical groves where sunshine dances over the tree canopy, warming the forest floor.

The Nairobi Arboretum is an engaging journey, not just a spot to observe nature. During guided tours, interact with the on-site botanists to discover the mysteries of plant life. Discover the life cycle of butterflies, learn about the medicinal uses of local plants, and comprehend the delicate balance between wildlife and vegetation that maintains this biodiverse sanctuary.

When the sun sets, and the arboreal tapestry is bathed in a golden light, you may find it hard to leave this Eden-like haven. However, Nairobi's dynamic energy is waiting beyond its boundaries, guaranteeing that the Nairobi Arboretum is not a haven from the city but a peaceful ally. In this haven, the natural and the urban coexist.

The Boma Nairobi

- **Location: Red Cross Road South C, Bellevue, Off Mombasa Road, Nairobi 00100 Kenya**
- **Hotel class: 5-star Hotel**

The Boma Nairobi is a shining example of kind hospitality in the center of this energetic city, combining luxury with a deep sense of mission. Allow me to share a story that goes beyond the ordinary, where each visit serves as a springboard to stop human suffering, as a witness to the evolving narrative of this exceptional enterprise.

The Boma Nairobi is a sanctuary where the dedication to humanity is evident in every nook and cranny, not simply a five-star hotel. It skillfully combines first-rate hospitality with a greater purpose: funding the humanitarian efforts of the Kenya Red Cross Society (KRCS). This is not just a hotel; it's a haven where the only thing as warm as the welcome you get is the warmth of the people who work here.

Entering the foyer, which is furnished with contemporary elegance and African creativity, you are drawn into a narrative that extends beyond the space it occupies. The idea is simple yet profound: "hospitality with a conscience." Everything about the Hotel, from the luxurious rooms to the cutting-edge meeting space, is intended to pamper visitors and raise money for charitable causes that lessen suffering and provide hope to people in need.

The Boma Nairobi promises to have a beneficial influence and is more than just a place to relax. Every dollar made here serves as a vital funding source for KRCS's humanitarian endeavors, including anything from community development to disaster relief. Creating a sustainable model where visitors choose superior service to contribute to the greater good is as exciting as the expansive views from the Hotel's terrace.

Imagine enjoying the scent of freshly brewed coffee when you wake up, knowing that your pleasure is helping to strengthen underprivileged communities. The Boma Nairobi's culinary experiences are a feast for the spirit and the senses. Every dish, whether it be a delicious local meal or an exquisite foreign delicacy, has the taste of compassion.

The conference center is where ideas come together, partnerships flourish, and change takes root. It is an extension of The Boma Nairobi's dedication. Here, the purpose of business meetings is change rather than transaction. Every meeting, conference, and get-together brings good change into the world and things far beyond boardrooms.

The Panari Hotel

- **Location: Mombasa Road, Nairobi 00506, Kenya**
- **Hotel class: 5-star Hotel**

Upon entering this peaceful refuge, you are welcomed with 136 tastefully renovated rooms, each offering a cozy haven. However, the double-glazed windows that encircle a breathtaking panoramic work of art are what catches the eye. The magnificent Nairobi National Park opens out before you like a wild canvas, and the Nairobi Central Business District, which is only a short distance away yet a world apart, can be seen beyond those windows.

Permit me to reveal a charming secret that distinguishes The Panari Hotel: an ice paradise that defies the heat of the torrid region. Yes, it is home to the sole ice rink in East and Central Africa, in Kenya and my fellow travelers. Dance on the frozen surface, making memories as you spin and glide with childlike delight.

The story doesn't stop there; oh no, it takes you on a trip through food. Imagine the hotel's main restaurant, The Red Garnet, to have a symphony of tastes resonating through its hallways. Every meal is a work of art here, a synthesis of regional specialties and international cuisine.

And for those looking for a wild night out, go to the "Shooters and Dips Lounge" on the second level. It's the vibrant entertainment center on Mombasa Road, not simply a club. The night is yours to seize, the rhythms are contagious, and the atmosphere is infused with enthusiasm.

But fear not, my fellow fitness enthusiasts—your commitment will not falter. Look at The Dolphin Health Club, a contemporary haven where working out becomes an adventure. Imagine being in an area with cutting-edge equipment, where your heartbeat and willpower are in sync. After the workout:

- Unwind in the sauna.
- Bask in the warmth of the steam room.
- Maybe cool down in the indoor swimming pool.

Additionally, The Panari Hotel exposes its sizable conference space for business-minded people. A collaborative canvas where invention flourishes, and ideas are allowed to flow freely. Not only is the area large, but it's also a loom of opportunities just waiting to be weaved.

Now, see this oasis as the starting point of your adventure rather than merely a spot to retire to. When it occurs, you don't have to worry about your ride since the Hotel has a spacious, safe parking area that can accommodate up to 450 automobiles while you're away.

TOP ATTRACTIONS
Nairobi National Park

Nairobi National Park is a refuge that is next to Kenya's busy metropolis and is a monument to how well urban life and wild nature coexist. Consider this: The spectacular grandeur of East Africa's animals is captured in a natural paradise only a short 15-minute drive from Nairobi's central business district.

Nairobi National Park, home to a varied range of flora and animals, is a magnificent 117 square kilometers nestled against the background of the city skyline. One of its distinguishing qualities is its close proximity to the city center, making it one of the world's most accessible national parks.

The park is one of Kenya's earliest conservation zones and was created in 1946, making it significant historically. Originally established as a barrier to prevent urban growth and to save the local fauna, it has transformed into an essential ecosystem that supports public education and environmental preservation.

One of its most recognizable characteristics is the view of the park's vast grassland and the silhouettes of Nairobi's skyscrapers. There is nothing like this bizarre experience anywhere else on Earth because of the contrast between natural nature and the urban jungle. Imagine a scene out of a fairytale, with the city skyline serving as a dramatic background and herds of zebras, giraffes, and wildebeests roaming freely in the foreground.

Nairobi National Park showcases the remarkable biodiversity of East Africa with its diverse array of species. The savannah is home to lions, cheetahs, leopards, and calmly grazing buffalo and rhinoceros. With over 400 kinds of birds identified, including secretary birds, crowned cranes, and ostriches, the park is also a birdwatcher's delight.

The chance to go on a safari experience without leaving the city boundaries is one of the pleasures of a trip to Nairobi National Park. With the background of vast grasslands and acacia trees, game drives in the park provide an immersive experience that lets visitors view the beauties of the animal life.

Nairobi National Park is home to various fascinating animals and is a center for environmental study and teaching. Within the park, the Ivory Burning Site Monument honors Kenya's dedication to the battle against the illicit ivory trade. The educational initiatives of the park are designed to increase public awareness of conservation and the precarious balance between human growth and the preservation of natural environments.

David Sheldrick Wildlife Trust

Founded in 1977 by Dr. Dame Daphne Sheldrick, the DSWT represents a steadfast dedication to protecting wildlife. Her late husband, David Sheldrick, was a well-known biologist and the first Warden of Tsavo East National Park. The trust's goal is simple yet profound: to save, heal, and eventually reintegrate orphaned elephants into the wild.

The DSWT, on the border of Nairobi National Park, provides a unique environment where the sounds of the natural world blend with the rhythms of urban life. Thanks to its advantageous position, the trust is able to react quickly to rescue operations. It often saves the lives of elephants suffering from poaching, habitat destruction, or conflict between humans and animals.

The newborn elephants' quiet trumpets and rustling motions welcome guests as they approach the trust, each serving as a symbol of the organization's commitment. The Nursery, where abandoned elephants find comfort under the careful eyes of a group of keepers acting as surrogate parents, is the center of DSWT. In addition to food, the pachyderm babies here get the affection and emotional support essential to their well-being.

The Creative Orphans' Project, which focuses on rehabilitating elephants to prepare them for a life back in the wild, is a cornerstone of the DSWT's success. The elephants go into reintegration units in protected wilderness locations as they become bigger, picking up important skills from their wild counterparts.

Observing the daily mud baths is a fantastic experience for visitors to the DSWT, and it goes beyond simple entertainment. Elephants' social and physical growth largely relies on the mud baths, where they enjoy the warm, Kenyan soil's healing properties and playful friendship.

The commitment of the trust goes beyond elephants. It actively participates in community engagement, environmental protection, and anti-poaching campaigns. The David Sheldrick Wildlife Trust proves the relationship between community, the wild, and conservation.

Beyond the obvious effects, the trust continues the vision of the late David Sheldrick, based on a great regard for the natural world and an awareness of the delicate balance between human habitation and the wilderness. The DSWT welcomes people to participate in a worldwide effort to safeguard and preserve these amazing animals for future generations, in addition to seeing the tenacity of orphaned elephants.

Giraffe Centre

There's a calmness about the Giraffe Centre that permeates the busy metropolis beyond its doors as soon as you enter. The African Fund for Endangered Wildlife (AFEW) founded the facility in 1979, and its primary emphasis was on the Rothschild's giraffe, which is critically endangered. These days, it serves as a haven for these elegant animals as well as an educational hub committed to promoting a better knowledge of wildlife protection.

The Rothschild's giraffes, the tallest inhabitants of the Giraffe Center, are its main attraction. These gentle giants walk freely inside the vast grounds of the facility, their characteristics unique and graceful. There's an air of reciprocal interest; they stretch out their long necks to ask questions as you get closer, creating a remarkable bond between guests and these amazing animals.

The ability to participate in a unique and unforgettable experience—feeding the giraffes—is a highlight of each visit. You can feel the silky lips of these beautiful creatures as they graciously accept your gift when you hold specially designed pellets in your palm. It's a bridge between species, a moment of connection that leaves a lasting impression on the heart.

Apart from offering up-close experiences with giraffes, the Giraffe Centre is dedicated to teaching about the environment. The on-site Nature Trail offers visitors an immersive experience through the verdant surroundings while educating them about the local wildlife and vegetation. The significance of wildlife conservation is explored in educational programs and guided excursions, with an emphasis on the need to safeguard Kenya's natural heritage.

The goal of the Giraffe Center goes beyond its walls; with a range of outreach initiatives, it engages the surrounding community. By promoting environmental stewardship and accountability, the center actively advances the general objective of sustainable coexistence between people and animals.

The Giraffe Centre calls to people looking for more than simply a safari—that is, a profound relationship with Kenya's animals.

Nestled within Nairobi's metropolitan vastness, its position serves as a painful reminder of the difficult balance that must be struck between growth and the preservation of the natural world's treasures.

Karen Blixen Museum

The old home of Karen Blixen, who resided on the estate from 1914 until 1931, is now the museum. The house has been kept intact to evoke the era in which Karen Blixen lived, complete with its unique architectural appeal. Every part of the room appears to whisper stories about her love of the country, her adventurous personality, and the enthralling tales she wove.

The Karen Blixen Museum's charm goes beyond its exquisite architecture. The large grounds around the home whisk guests away to the serene settings Blixen captured on paper. An exquisite scene is created by tall jacaranda trees, expansive lawns, and the shadow of acacia trees, which encourage introspection and a sense of oneness with the natural world.

Seeing Blixen's personal belongings and the objects that ornamented her everyday life is one of the museum's attractions. Every object she had, from the ancient furniture that saw her adventures come and go to the old-fashioned typewriter she used to write her moving stories, is a window into the past.

Blixen's paintings and drawings are also displayed in the museum, providing insight into her creative pursuits. Her artworks provide a visual accompaniment to her literary legacy, capturing her astute observation of the local culture and surroundings in striking detail.

The Karen Blixen Museum is a living record of Kenya's colonial past and of Blixen's unwavering spirit, not just a static exhibition of relics. Wandering about the grounds, one can practically hear Blixen's voice echoing, feel the rhythm of the once-flourishing coffee plantation, and be in awe of the expansive vistas that served as her creative inspiration.

In addition to its historical relevance, the museum hosts events, exhibits, and educational activities as a cultural hub. It is a memorial to Blixen's love of storytelling, sensitivity to cultural differences, and steadfast devotion to the Kenyan environment.

The museum in Karen provides an immersive experience for anybody who wants to explore the strands of Karen Blixen's heritage. It's more than simply a physical location—it's a literary encounter, a historical expedition, and an investigation of the human soul.

CULTURAL EXPERIENCES
Maasai Market

Imagine the following: the perfume of leather, the beat of traditional Maasai melodies, and the vivid colors of jewelry with meticulous beadwork fill the air. The Maasai Market is a mobile exhibition that graces several areas in Nairobi, making it accessible to residents and visitors keen to see Kenyan workmanship's genuine beauty.

This bustling marketplace may be seen along the streets of major hubs such as City Hall, upscale shopping centers, or even the Village Market courtyard on any given day. A new location is available daily, revealing various handmade items.

Beaded jewelry, a Maasai hallmark, is the lifeblood of the Maasai Market. A plethora of vibrant bracelets, necklaces, and earrings entice, with every bead telling a tale of custom, individuality, and craftsmanship. The Maasai are renowned for their meticulous beading; they often use vivid colors and complex designs representing several facets of their culture, such as age and social standing.

The traditional Maasai shukas' red and blue colors draw your attention as you go through the market. These colorful, patterned blankets are more than textiles; they represent the Maasai people's comfort and nomadic past. Several tourists consider these shukas to be priceless mementos, enveloping themselves in a fragment of Maasai heritage.

Another bright spot in the Maasai Market constellation is leatherwork. Sandals, purses, and belts are expertly crafted by artisans, expressing the Maasai people's strong bond with their pastoral lifestyle. Every item is proof of the tenacity and inventiveness of a people who have prospered in the harsh environments of East Africa.

Products aren't the only thing on the market; there is also cultural exchange. Talking with the Maasai merchants gives you the chance to hear their tales, discover more about their art, and maybe even laugh a little. Not only is haggling acceptable, but bargaining is an essential component of the transaction—a dance between the buyer and the seller, a shared enjoyment of the artistic expression on exhibit.

The Maasai Market's flexibility and agility are what set it apart. It travels rather than staying in one place, spreading its colorful vitality across Nairobi. It embodies the spirit of the Maasai, who are always adapting to change and clinging to their traditions.

Kazuri Beads Women's Cooperative

Established in 1975 by the late Lady Susan Wood, an Englishwoman with a strong emotional connection with the Kenyan people, Kazuri Beads was born out of the financial struggles of the region's single mothers. Simply put, "Kazuri" means "small and beautiful" in Swahili, which is a good description of the magnificent clay beads made by hand and have come to represent this cooperative.

The fact that each bead is individually molded and painted by hand, creating a one-of-a-kind piece of art, really sets Kazuri Beads apart. You can see the women's deft hands at work as you stroll about the cooperative, molding clay into beautiful designs and giving each bead life with vivid hues drawn from the scenery of Kenya.

However, Kazuri Beads is a sanctuary of empowerment and a location of exquisite workmanship. Women from underprivileged backgrounds, especially single moms, are the cooperative's main employees. Through their employment, they can provide a steady source of income for their families. Kazuri Beads shines a light on the power and creativity that come from the hands of these artists, providing possibilities for women in a world when such opportunities might be scarce.

The cooperative fosters a feeling of community among its members and offers jobs. These ladies share a feeling of purpose, humor, and tales while working together. It's a sisterhood that extends beyond the sewing table, a structure of encouragement and empowerment.

There's more to discover at the Kazuri Beads workshop than simply beads. The artists also work with clay, producing various goods, such as beautiful animal figurines and elaborately patterned dishes. Every artwork showcases Kenya's rich cultural legacy via a blend of modern craftsmanship and customs.

A rainbow of hues welcomes you when you enter the Kazuri Beads shop. These distinctive beads decorate necklaces, bracelets, and earrings that beckon, each item expressing a tale of artistry, tenacity, and Kenya's colorful personality. Buying a Kazuri product is an investment in the livelihoods of these gifted women, not just a lovely accessory.

In addition to winning over those who value handcrafted art, Kazuri Beads has achieved recognition on a global scale. Its goods aren't limited to Nairobi; they've found homes all over the globe and have come to represent Kenyan women's empowerment and workmanship.

Bomas of Kenya

Even the term "Bomas" comes from the Swahili word for "homesteads," and visiting this cultural haven is like joining a collective hug of Kenya's many tribes. The admirable goal of the Bomas of Kenya's establishment in 1971 was to conserve, develop, and present the nation's rich cultural legacy.

Entering Bomas will take you to a world where song, dance, and tradition unite to convey the stories of 42 ethnic groups in Kenya. A colorful show featuring the beauty and passion of traditional

Kenyan dances takes place in the main auditorium, which is decorated with traditional African décor.

Visitors have a front-row seat to the vibrant pulse of Kenyan culture as they are enthralled with the drumming, rhythmic chanting, and vibrant swirl of costumes. Every performance tells a tale using dance and rhythm, describing the customs, festivals, and day-to-day activities of the many people who inhabit Kenya.

Bomas offers more than just a stage experience. Explore the re-created homesteads, each representing a distinct ethnic group, to learn about the distinctive crafts, architectural designs, and ways of life that set each community apart. Interact with the artists as they demonstrate their customary weaving, woodcarving, and beading, preserving the ancestors' crafts handed down through the ages.

It would be impossible to discuss Bomas without bringing up the mesmerizing performance of traditional music. From the soul-stirring pounding of African drums to the beautiful melodies of stringed instruments, the talented performers display various instruments. The music is a cultural symphony that connects with Kenya's history and culture, going beyond just pleasure.

TRANSPORTATION WITHIN THE CITY
Public Transportation

Nairobi has a wide range of reasonably priced public transportation options. Buses and matatus are the most often used public transportation options.

Shared minibusses, or matatus, have a maximum capacity of 14 people. Due to their affordability and availability on most main highways, they are the most widely used mode of public transit in Nairobi. However, matatus are known to be unsafe and may be packed and unpleasant.

Matatus may be replaced by buses, which are safer and more pleasant. They follow the same routes as matatus and are run by public and commercial enterprises. In addition to being less expensive than cabs, buses may also be slower and more congested, particularly during rush hour.

In Nairobi, there are trains in addition to matatus and buses. Although it is not as large as the bus system and is relatively new, the rail system provides useful transportation to and from the airport.

Here are some tips for using public transportation in Nairobi:
- Get ready to barter. You must bargain with the driver to get the fare while riding in a matatu. Since there are no fixed rates for matatus, it's essential to be ready to haggle.

- Possess little bills. Cash is the sole form of payment accepted by matatus and buses; thus having tiny notes is essential.
- Pay attention to your surroundings. Nairobi's public transit system may be congested and disorganized, so it's important to be mindful of your surroundings and take safety measures to protect yourself from pickpockets and other thieves.
- Have patience. It's crucial to be organized and patient while using Nairobi's public transit system since it may sometimes be erratic and sluggish.

Here is a list of the different types of public transportation available in Nairobi:
- Matatus
- Buses
- Trains
- Taxis
- Ride-hailing apps

Car Rentals and Taxis

Car Rentals

Nairobi is home to many domestic and foreign vehicle rental agencies. The majority of large hotels and airports hire cars. Check rates and thoroughly read the terms and conditions before renting a vehicle.

Some popular car rental companies in Nairobi include:
- Avis
- Budget
- Hertz
- Europcar
- Sixt
- Rent a Car Kenya
- Express Impress Car Hire Ltd.
- Metro Car Hire Services

Taxis

Another well-liked mode of transportation in Nairobi is taxis. Outside of hotels, airports, and other significant sites are taxi stands. Before getting into a taxi, you must haggle over a fee with the driver.

Some popular taxi companies in Nairobi include:
- City Cab
- Safaricom Cabs
- Uber
- Bolt

Here are some tips for renting a car or taking a taxi in Nairobi:

- Reserve your rental vehicle in advance. This is particularly crucial if you go during the busiest time of year.
- Before hiring a vehicle, thoroughly review the terms and conditions and compare rates.
- Make sure your foreign driver's license is up to date.
- Before you get in the cab, haggle over a fee with the driver.
- To protect yourself from pickpockets and other thieves, consider your surroundings and adopt safety measures.

OUTDOOR ADVENTURES
Ngong Hills Hike

The Ngong Hills, with its peaks soaring beyond the skies, watch over Nairobi from their seductive nest, just a short drive from the city's bustling center. This journey, a pilgrimage for hikers and environment lovers, is more than just a walk—it's a connection with the wild beauty that Kenya so kindly grants to those seeking it.

The trailhead, a portal to a world where the exceptional emerges and the commonplace vanishes, is where the journey starts. The fresh air is perfumed with wildflowers as you climb, and songbirds accompany you. The rolling landscape shows off its treasures: panoramas that never stop, hills that test the brave, and valleys that hold secrets and create an unending canvas of horizons.

The Ngong Hills have many peaks, each having a distinct personality and attraction. At the top, the terrain opens below you, revealing a mix of savannah plains, undulating hills, and the far-off silhouette of Nairobi. It's a split second when the heartbeat of nature becomes your own, and the city's pulse seems a planet away.

Look out for the Maasai herders who live in these highlands as you follow the routes. Their presence gives the trip an additional cultural depth and serves as a reminder that the Ngong Hills are a canvas on which human tales are painted as much as a geographical wonder.

The Out of Africa vista, made famous by Karen Blixen's novel, is one of the route's most famous locations. Here, the Ngong Hills play a character role in the story of Africa's attraction, and the scenery perfectly embodies the spirit of an ancient period.

The Ngong Hills Hike is a sensory immersion experience rather than a physical activity. Allow the expansive vistas to leave an impression on your mind, the sensation of the ground under your feet and the sound of grass rustling in the air. Every stride is a rhythmic journey towards self-discovery, a dance with the natural world.

The Ngong Hills change as the day grows longer and the sun sets. The sunset's golden colors paint the scenery in warm tones, giving it an ethereal, enchanting shine. The trek ends with a symphony of hues, a crescendo to an experience that will always be carved in your heart and thoughts.

Karura Forest

This urban forest reserve, which covers an area of more than 1,000 hectares, is evidence of Nairobi's dedication to protecting its natural legacy despite the fast-paced pace of the city.

Imagine yourself in a lush paradise just a short distance from the concrete jungle. The Karura Forest is a haven for nature lovers, tired city dwellers, and daring explorers. The trip starts at the imposing main gate, which serves as a doorway from the bustle of the city into a peaceful world of pathways, tall trees, and the melodic sound of birdcalls.

Karura's landscape is breathtaking, and its rich past contributes to its allure. The woodland, formerly part of Colonel Eric Dutton's expansive estate, was threatened by deterioration and land grabs. But then, in a stunning turn of events in the early 1990s, the Green Belt Movement, spearheaded by the renowned Wangari Maathai, and environmental activists banded together to protect this sanctuary from invasion. You are now strolling along a route made possible by the commitment of individuals who battled bravely to preserve this natural gem as you meander through the trails.

One of its most distinctive characteristics is the extensive system of well-designated pathways that winds through Karura Forest. Every step you take transports you to a world where towering trees form a canopy above, sunshine filters through the leaves, and the air is filled with the earthy aroma of the forest floor—whether you choose the well-known Wangari Maathai or the magnificent waterfall routes.

Another element of magic is added by the Karura River, which flows through the forest's center like lifeblood. Its winding road leads to the captivating Karura Waterfall, a hidden treasure nestled in the embrace of the surrounding vegetation. The sound and sight of the water falling form a symphony that touches the soul, providing the ideal setting for introspection and renewal.

The Forest Reserve has an elaborate cave system for the more daring among us, with the Bat Cave serving as a reminder of the geological marvels of the forest. The chilly, damp air and stalagmites that dangle like old chandeliers make the investigation more mysterious.

Karura Forest is a refuge for a wide variety of plants and animals and a paradise for hikers and environment enthusiasts. The chance to see a range of bird species, from the colorful sunbirds to the magnificent African Crowned Eagle, is a treat for birdwatchers. Various fauna, such as duikers, sykes monkeys, and bushbucks, call the forest home, giving the urban scene a hint of the wild.

Karura Forest, however, represents community involvement and sustainable living and is more than simply a place to escape to nature. The forest encourages residents and tourists to care for this priceless ecosystem by holding educational events, planting campaigns, and tree-planting activities.

Hot Air Balloon Safari

The hot air balloon transforms into a dream-catcher as the sun rises, gliding above Nairobi's scenery with ease. The adventure starts in the gentle embrace of the early air, with the lucky people participating in this flying adventure exchanging quiet thrills. The canvas underneath opens out, displaying the unadulterated splendor that characterizes the Kenyan wilderness—a patchwork quilt of greens and gold.

The view that the Hot Air Balloon Safari offers, in addition to its height, makes it so appealing. Nairobi National Park has a new significance with its vast grassland and recognizable acacia trees. The animals below seem like a living tapestry from this vantage point: grazing herds of zebras, elegant giraffes, and maybe the majestic outline of a far-off lion, all involved in the ageless dance of nature.

The only sound to break the stillness on the voyage is the sporadic whoosh of the burner's flame. It's a calm ballet, an ethereal dance that reaches from the sky's surface to the ground. The pilot, an accomplished aviator, leads this quiet journey, ensuring every eye is treated to an amazing view.

The closeness to wildlife is one of the unrivaled attractions of Nairobi's Hot Air Balloon Safari. You become an invisible observer as you softly glide over the terrain, giving you a unique perspective on creatures in their natural environment. The experience is breathtaking yet humble simultaneously, demonstrating the careful balancing act between Nairobi's metropolitan pulse and the natural rhythms of the surrounding area. The metropolis of Nairobi itself is transformed into a composition of contrasts as the balloon flies over the canvas with elegance. The coexistence of the nature reserve and the urban expansion creates a story of peaceful coexistence. A striking illustration of Nairobi's distinct personality is the contrast between the city's central business district and the wild splendor of the national park.

The Hot Air Balloon Safari ends with a leisurely descent, with the ground rising to greet the passengers as they get from their aerial vehicle. But the experience leaves a lasting impression, a kaleidoscope of recollections that last long after the burner's flames go out.

NIGHTLIFE

Trendy Bars and Clubs

Nairobi, the capital of Kenya, is a vibrant city with a diverse nightlife. There are many trendy bars and clubs in Nairobi, depending on your taste in music and atmosphere.

Here are a few of the most popular trendy bars and clubs in Nairobi:

- A rooftop bar called Skylux Lounge is situated in Nairobi's Westlands district. It provides a vibrant environment and breathtaking views of the downtown skyline. It's fun to dance, sip drinks, and mingle at Skylux Lounge.
- Speakeasy-style bar The Alchemist is situated in Nairobi's Kilimani district. It provides a special, private drinking experience. numerous house mixologists' trademark beverages are among the numerous options available at The Alchemist.
- Nairobi's Westlands district is home to the well-known nightclub K1 Klub House. It plays various music, such as techno, house, and hip-hop. A fantastic location to dance the night away is K1 Klub House.
- Nairobi's Westlands district is home to the upscale nightclub B-CLUB Nairobi. It plays a wide range of music,

such as electronic, hip-hop, and house. A terrific spot to see and be seen in Nairobi is B-CLUB.

- Brew Bistro & Lounge is a well-liked destination for both residents and visitors. In addition to a delectable cuisine menu, it serves a large assortment of beers, wines, and drinks. Brew Bistro & Lounge is a fantastic spot to decompress and chill with pals.

Live Music Venues

Nairobi has a thriving live music scene, with venues catering to various tastes. Here are a few of the most popular live music venues in Nairobi:

- Tamambo Bar & Grill is a well-liked location for both visitors and residents. In addition to a large assortment of food and beverages, it has live music most nights of the week. You can catch various local and international musicians playing at Tamambo Bar & Grill.
- Famous for its grilled meats and live music, The Carnivore is a restaurant that has gained international recognition. Most evenings of the week, musicians play on the spacious outdoor stage of The Carnivore. The Carnivore is a fantastic venue for dining and live entertainment.
- The public can join the exclusive Muthaiga Country Club on certain weeknights. The club has a large ballroom where

musicians often play. The elegant Muthaiga Country Club is a fantastic venue for live performances.
- Dagoz Bar is a well-liked location for both residents and visitors. In addition to a large assortment of food and beverages, it has live music most nights of the week. You can see a range of local musicians playing at Dagoz Bar.

These are just a few of the many live music venues in Nairobi. With so many options, you are sure to find a place that is perfect for you.

Here are some additional tips for finding a live music venue in Nairobi:

- Consult the concierge at your hotel for suggestions.
- Examine internet reviews.
- Check your local magazines and newspapers for listings of live music.
- Find out where local musicians are playing by following them on social media.
- In some places, be prepared to pay a cover fee.

Night Safaris

Nairobi's night safari offers an exciting and distinctive opportunity to see the city's animals waking up after dark. Nairobi National Park is one of the greatest sites in Kenya to go on a night safari, and it's just outside the city.

Numerous nocturnal creatures, such as lions, leopards, hyenas, and rhinos, may be seen in the park. You may get up close and personal with these creatures as they hunt and eat on a night safari. Most night safaris occur in open-air safari vehicles, giving you a full 360-degree view of the park. The guides can identify animals in the dark because of the strong spotlights installed in the cars.

The majority of night safaris endure three to four hours. Your knowledgeable guide will educate you about the park's fauna throughout the safari. Additionally, you can record and capture images of the creatures.

Here are some tips for booking a night safari in Nairobi:

- If you are going at the busiest time of year, make your safari reservations well in advance.
- Before making a safari reservation, compare costs and read reviews.
- Select a trustworthy safari operator.
- Make sure the vehicle you choose for your safari is open-air.
- It may become chilly in the park at night, so pack thick clothing.
- To record the event, carry a camera or video camera.

Here are some of the best places to book a night safari in Nairobi:

- Natural World Safaris

- African Spice Safari
- Bonfire Adventures
- Explore Kenya Safaris
- Acacia Expeditions

EVENTS AND FESTIVALS

Nairobi International Trade Fair

The Nairobi International Trade Fair is an eye-popping rainbow of hues, noises, and sensations. Imagine vast display exhibits filled with cattle, agricultural products, equipment, and cutting-edge technology, painting an enthralling picture of Kenya's economic might. Farmers, business owners, financiers, and consumers come together at the fair to form a melting pot that shapes the country's economic fabric.

The fair strongly emphasizes agriculture, highlighting the fertility of Kenya's land and the inventiveness of its farmers. The agricultural industry is alive and well in every square inch of the show grounds, which include everything from the newest innovations in animal breeding to crop production. Farmers share information, professionals present cutting-edge technology, and the general public learns about the nuances of sustainable agricultural methods.

However, the Nairobi International Trade Fair embraces the industrial environment with just as much zeal as the fields. Modern equipment, creative fixes, and game-changing technology stand tall, inviting businesspeople and financiers to participate in Kenya's industrial revolution. The fair is an intellectual marketplace where the spirit of invention mingles with manufacturing demands.

The trade show's cultural tapestry is just as fascinating. Kenya is characterized by its diverse cultural mosaic, seen via traditional dances, music, and creative exhibitions. Viewers are more than simply participants in a peaceful dance that crosses borders and unites communities; they are part of a celebration of variety and harmony.

Jamhuri Park comes alive with a colorful nighttime carnival as the sun sets. The night comes alive with music and entertainment, and the air is filled with the fragrances of delicious local cuisine. It's an opportunity to relax, enjoy the tastes of Kenyan food, and take in the festive atmosphere that fills the fairgrounds.

The Nairobi International Trade Fair is important for promoting partnerships and collaborations in addition to its economic and cultural aspects. It's a hub where companies meet, ideas emerge, and bonds strengthen. The networking possibilities are just as varied as the displays, resulting in a synergy long after the fair finishes.

Blankets & Wine Festival

Imagine a broad, verdant countryside, a sea of colorful blankets laid out like a patchwork quilt, and a day full of sunshine. Every time the Blankets & Wine Festival comes to Nairobi, the Ngong Racecourse is transformed into a kaleidoscope of colors and noises. This is the sight that takes place. Since its founding in 2008, this festival has become a must-go-to event, a gathering place for fans of music art, and those looking for a special combination of entertainment and friendship.

Unquestionably, the music—a soul-stirring roster that cuts across boundaries and genres—is the beating core of Blankets & Wine. The event curates a varied musical tapestry, ranging from addictive pop beats to jazz melodies and mesmerizing Afrobeat rhythms that pulse through the air. Renowned national and international performers adorn the stage, creating a soul-stirring immersive experience.

However, Blankets & Wine is a cultural feast that honors the diverse range of Kenyan talent rather than only being a music festival. The festival grounds come to life with pop-up art pieces beyond the main stage, exhibiting the skills of regional sculptors and visual artists. Visitors are encouraged to investigate, engage, and fully submerge in the vivid inventiveness that characterizes Nairobi's dynamic artistic landscape.

Blankets & Wine's menu items are a gourmet adventure unto itself. The event is transformed into a gastronomic kaleidoscope by the variety of food exhibitors, who provide everything from delicious local street cuisine to exquisite worldwide gourmet experiences. The aromas of grilled meats, exotic spices, and the enticing perfume of freshly brewed coffee fill the air, attesting to the festival's dedication to pleasing the palette in addition to the senses of hearing.

Blankets & Wine is distinct because of its atmosphere. In addition to sitting in rows of chairs, attendees recline on blankets and cushions, fostering a laid-back and social environment. Under the common roof of the Nairobi sky, the event fosters a sense of community where strangers become friends and friends become family.

Blankets & Wine turns into a nighttime extravaganza as the sun sets. The celebration continues late into the night with the festival's after-hours events, which include dance acts and DJ sets. The moon becomes a quiet observer of the happiness permeating the festival grounds.

Blankets & Wine is not only a one-time event; rather, it is a cultural movement that has been ingrained in Nairobi's culture. It captures the essence of this city's unique blend of innovation, variety, and togetherness. Every festival iteration is part of a bigger tale about the convergence of music, art, and community on the verdant grounds of Ngong Racecourse.

Maasai Mara Marathon

Imagine the following scene: the sun rises over the huge savannah, bathing the golden meadows in a warm light. Hearts racing with excitement, runners worldwide assemble at the starting line against this breathtaking canvas. Not only is the Maasai Mara Marathon a physical challenge, but it's also an adventure through the wild grandeur of the Maasai Mara, one of the Seven Wonders of globally and a UNESCO World Heritage Site.

The brilliant hues of Maasai culture and the raw, unadulterated spirit of the African bush are woven together like a tapestry throughout the marathon course. Running through the terrain home to the Great Wildebeest Migration, an annual natural extravaganza that takes place across the Mara River, runners are more than just participants as they pound the trails.

It is impossible to discuss the Maasai Mara Marathon without exploring the diverse cultural heritage of the Maasai people. The marathon celebrates their culture, bringing together traditional dance, music, and the characteristic red shukas, beaded jewelry, and shoes that are unique to the Maasai people. The melodic rhythms of Maasai songs reverberate, producing a symphony that echoes with the beating of feet.

The Maasai Mara Marathon is unique because it is dedicated to environmental preservation. The marathon serves as a forum to promote community empowerment and animal conservation in addition to being an athletic event. The marathon's proceeds fund programs that protect the Maasai Mara's distinctive ecosystems and assist the local people in coexisting peacefully with animals.

Along the marathon course, participants come to see the wild residents of Maasai Mara:

- Elephants sauntering over the grasslands
- Giraffes munching elegantly on acacia leaves
- The elusive big cats lurking in the shadows

As a result, the marathon turns into a dance of symbiosis between people and the natural world, demonstrating the perfect balance that characterizes this extraordinary environment.

The Maasai Mara Marathon finish line is more than a landmark; it's a celebration of victory and the pinnacle of the human spirit set against one of the most breathtaking backdrops on earth. A feeling of achievement fills runners as they cross the finish line—not only from finishing a marathon but also from knowing they are part of a movement that embodies the Maasai Mara's pulse.

SHOPPING AND DINING

Unique Markets and Shops

Masai Market

- Location: Maasai Market Road, Langata, Nairobi, Kenya
- Open every day from 8:00 AM till 7:00 PM.
- What to find: The Masai Market is a popular tourist destination known for its colorful Maasai handicrafts, including jewelry, clothing, and beaded items. The market also sells souvenirs like keychains, magnets, and postcards.

Kibera Market

- Location: Kibera Drive, Kibera, Nairobi, Kenya
- Open hours: 7:00 AM - 7:00 PM, daily
- What to find: Kibera is the largest informal settlement in Africa, and its market is a bustling hive of activity. The market sells everything from fresh produce to used clothes to electronics. It is a great place to experience the real Nairobi and to find unique souvenirs.

Uhuru Market

- Location: Kenyatta Avenue, Nairobi, Kenya
- Open hours: 8:00 AM - 7:00 PM, daily
- What to find: Uhuru Market is a large indoor market that sells various goods, including food, clothing, electronics,

and household items. It is a great place to find bargains and to experience the local culture.

Yaya Centre

- Location: Argwings Kodhek Road, Nairobi, Kenya
- Open hours: 10:00 AM - 7:00 PM, daily
- What to find: Yaya Centre is a modern shopping mall that houses a variety of international and local brands. It is a great place to find clothes, shoes, accessories, and electronics. The mall also has a food court with various restaurants and cafes.

The Village Market

- Location: Limuru Road, Nairobi, Kenya
- Open every day from 9:00 AM till 7:00 PM.
- What to find: The Village Market is an open-air shopping mall with various shops, restaurants, and cafes. It is a great place to find unique items, such as handmade jewelry, clothing, and home decor. The mall also has a children's play area and a cinema.

Nairobi Gallery

- Location: Raphta Road, Nairobi, Kenya
- Open hours: 9:00 AM - 5:00 PM, Tuesday to Saturday

- What to find: Nairobi Gallery is a contemporary art gallery that showcases the work of Kenyan and international artists. The gallery also holds seminars and events.

Duka la Jambo
- Location: Kitengela Road, Karen, Nairobi, Kenya
- Open hours: 9:00 AM - 5:00 PM, Monday to Saturday
- What to find: Duka la Jambo is a social enterprise that sells handmade products from Kenya and other African countries. Artisans make the products from disadvantaged communities, and the proceeds from sales go back to supporting these communities.

Culinary Delights in Nairobi

Nairobi is a melting pot of cultures, and this is reflected in its culinary scene. From traditional Kenyan dishes to international cuisine, there is something for everyone to enjoy in Nairobi. Here are a few of the city's culinary delights:

- Popular in Kenya, Nyama Choma means "roasted meat" in Swahili. Usually, marinated beef, goat, or lamb is used, which is roasted over charcoal. A starchy meal made from maize flour called ugali is often served with nyama choma.
- In Kenya, ugali is a staple diet. Made with water and maize flour, it is usually eaten with a stew or sauce. Ugali is a

well-liked option for breakfast or supper and a wonderful source of energy and carbs.

- Collard greens and tomatoes are combined to make the Kenyan delicacy Sukuma Wiki. It is a well-liked side dish often served with rice or ugali. Sukuma Wiki is a low-fat, low-calorie meal and an excellent source of vitamins and minerals.
- Mashed potatoes, green beans, and maize are the main ingredients of the Kenyan meal irio ndogo. It is a well-liked side dish often served with ugali or nyama choma. An excellent source of vitamins, minerals, and carbs is irio ndogo.
- Boiling or steaming green bananas is called matoke. They are a well-liked side dish often served with fish or pork. Matoke is an excellent source of minerals, vitamins, and carbs.
- A Kenyan meal called gethiri is prepared with cooked beans and maize. It is a well-liked side dish often served with meat or veggies. Githeri is a healthy source of fiber, protein, and carbs.
- Mandazi, a popular snack or morning meal, are fried doughnuts from Kenya that are then covered with sugar. Mandazi are often served with tea or coffee and are fluffy and airy.

- Popular in Kenya and other East African nations is chapati, a flatbread. It is usually cooked on a grill and is prepared using wheat flour and water. Chapati is often served with stew or curry.
- A triangle pastry stuffed with meat or veggies is called a sambusa. In Kenya, it's a common appetizer or snack. Usually, sambusa are baked or fried.
- In Kenya, chai is a popular tea kind. Sugar, milk, and black tea are the ingredients. Usually served hot, chai is enjoyed with foods like chapati or mandazi.

Popular Restaurants and Cafés

Restaurants

Carnivore Restaurant:

- Location: Langata Road, Langata, Nairobi, Kenya
- Open hours: 12:30 PM - 11:00 PM, daily
- What to find: Carnivore Restaurant is a world-famous restaurant known for its grilled meats and live music. The restaurant has a large outdoor terrace where guests can enjoy a variety of meats, including beef, goat, lamb, and ostrich. There are several sides and sauces to go with the meats. Carnivore Restaurant also has a full bar and a wine list.

Tamambo Karen Blixen Coffee Garden:

- Location: Karen Blixen Road, Karen, Nairobi, Kenya
- Open hours: 7:00 AM - 10:00 PM, daily
- What to find: Tamambo Karen Blixen Coffee Garden is a popular restaurant and coffee shop on the grounds of the Karen Blixen Museum. The restaurant offers a variety of Kenyan and international dishes, including salads, sandwiches, burgers, and pasta. The coffee shop serves a variety of coffees, teas, and pastries. Tamambo Karen Blixen Coffee Garden also has a beautiful garden terrace where guests can relax and enjoy their meal or drink.

The Talisman:

- Location: Westlands Road, Westlands, Nairobi, Kenya
- Daily hours of operation: 12:00 PM to 11:00 PM
- What to find: The Talisman is a popular restaurant and bar in the Westlands neighborhood of Nairobi. The restaurant offers a variety of international dishes, including sushi, pizza, and steak. The bar offers a selection of wines, beers, and cocktails. The Talisman also has a live music stage and a dance floor.

Cafés

About Thyme:

- Location: Riverside Drive, Westlands, Nairobi, Kenya
- Open hours: 7:00 AM - 10:00 PM, daily

- What to find: About Thyme is a popular café and restaurant in the Riverside neighborhood of Nairobi. The café offers a variety of coffees, teas, and pastries. The restaurant offers a variety of Kenyan and international dishes, including salads, sandwiches, and burgers. About Thyme also has a beautiful outdoor terrace where guests can relax and enjoy their meal or drink.

Artcaffe:
- Location: Various locations throughout Nairobi, Kenya
- Open hours: 7:00 AM - 10:00 PM, daily
- What to find: Artcaffe is a popular cafe chain in Nairobi. The cafes offer a variety of coffees, teas, and pastries. Artcaffe also offers a variety of light meals, such as sandwiches, salads, and wraps.

The Green House:
- Location: Waiyaki Way, Westlands, Nairobi, Kenya
- Open Monday through Saturday from 7:00 AM to 6:00 PM
- What to find: The Green House is a popular café in the Westlands neighborhood of Nairobi. The café offers a variety of coffees, teas, and pastries. The Green House also offers a variety of healthy breakfast and lunch options, such as yogurt parfaits, avocado toast, and salads. The café also has a beautiful garden terrace where guests can relax and enjoy their meal or drink.

DAY TRIPS FROM NAIROBI

Lake Naivasha

Set off on an expedition into the center of peace, where the air is filled with the delightful aroma of adventure, and the gently flowing waterways murmur quiet stories. A visit to Lake Naivasha, a freshwater treasure nestled in Kenya's Great Rift Valley, offers an extraordinary encounter with the natural world.

Excitement builds to a crescendo as you travel through the picturesque scenery on approach to Lake Naivasha. The lake's sparkling width opens out in front of you as the road winds through lush hills. The initial impression is a glimpse captured in time, a magnificent welcome foreshadowing the tranquility beyond.

Take a boat safari to start your journey, which is fascinating and reveals Lake Naivasha's mysteries. Sail over the calm waterways, while swarms of birds create a kaleidoscope of color in the sky. Through the papyrus-lined canals, the boat transforms into a means of exploration, unveiling the secret world of waterbucks, hippos, and the elusive African fish eagle. Every birdcall is a symphony reverberating over the vast open space, and every wave tells a tale.

Reach Crescent Island by mooring your boat and entering this haven, which resembles something out of a dream. Imagine a crescent-shaped sanctuary where zebras meander in a serene symphony of animals, giraffes gracefully reach for the treetops, and wildebeests graze in peace. This is a private dance with nature, where you are just a visitor in their realm; it's not a safari.

Lake Naivasha is a sanctuary for avian lovers, home to more than 400 different kinds of amazing birds. The air is filled with the different sounds and fluttering wings of these feathery dwellers, from the graceful African fish eagles to the exquisite flamingos. The lake's edges are surrounded by colorful water lilies, euphorbia, and acacia trees, which create a tapestry of hues that sways in the wind, appealing to those who like botany.

Enjoy a picnic by the lake as the noon sun casts a warm warmth over everything. Lay down a blanket among the acacia trees and enjoy a meal while the calm waters provide background music. It's more than simply a meal—it's a chance to connect with nature, a pause in time when the splendor of Lake Naivasha becomes a part of who you are.

An excursion to Hell's Gate National Park is a must for anyone with a spirit of adventure while visiting Lake Naivasha. Hike beside geothermal springs, across towering cliffs, and through stunning gorges to unleash your inner adventurer. The park's unusual terrain was so captivating that Disney used it to inspire "The Lion King," demonstrating its otherworldly appeal.

Amboseli National Park

Traveling from Nairobi to Amboseli is like traveling through a tapestry of shifting scenery. The pulsating urban bustle gives way to the steady hum of the road as you leave the city behind. With every mile, the suspense grows since one knows that a sanctuary where nature is dominant is just ahead.

As soon as you arrive, Mount Kilimanjaro's famous silhouette fills the sky with its beautiful shadow falling over Amboseli, Africa's tallest mountain silently watches over the park. It's an incredible sight that serves as a constant reminder of the majesty and unadulterated force of nature.

Entering Amboseli, the scenery opens out before you like a live painting. The horizon is filled with expansive grasslands scattered with acacia trees and laced with marshes home to a diverse array of birds. The sounds of zebras, wildebeests, and elephants—the real lords of this wilderness—trumpet through the air.

The elephants are undoubtedly the main attraction on any day excursion to Amboseli. Large herds of these magnificent animals are well-known in Amboseli, and seeing them against Kilimanjaro's background is an experience that will live in memory. Elephants are free to wander the savannah, their tusks glistening in the sunshine as they pass. This particular sight perfectly captures the essence of African animal protection.

As the day goes on, the safari cars wind through the park, exposing a fresh scene of animals at every bend. Zebra swarms weave over the grasslands, towering giraffes peruse the treetops, and distant herds of buffalo graze. Predators also find refuge in the park; lions rest under acacia trees, cheetahs stalk elegantly, and leopards, who may be hiding in the golden glory of dusk, may be seen.

It is impossible to discuss Amboseli without mentioning its bird inhabitants. With more than 400 species identified, the park is a birdwatcher's dream. Aerial eagles fly above, flamingos wade in the shallow waters, and vivid lilac-breasted rollers give bursts of color to the scenery.

A day excursion to Amboseli offers an insight into Maasai culture and animal viewing. The Maasai people have a symbiotic connection with the earth, as seen by their colorful clothing and beaded jewelry. A Maasai village tour provides an opportunity to interact with a community that coexists peacefully with the environment and a peek into their customs and dances.

Nairobi to Mombasa: A Coastal Adventure

The excitement of the beach adventure fills the air in Nairobi as the day starts. A leisurely early-morning trip of around 500 kilometers reveals the varying landscapes, from the bustling pace of Nairobi to the rolling hills leading to Mombasa, the seaside treasure.

The route stretches out like a ribbon as it winds across the Great Rift Valley, passing through stunning scenery that alludes to the country of East Africa's natural treasures. The smell of the Indian

Ocean fills the air as you descend, a mouthwatering precursor to the beachside retreat waiting for you.

When one arrives at Mombasa, the entry point to the Kenyan coast, one's senses are quickly taken over by another reality. Old Town entices with its historical beauty a maze of little lanes adorned with vintage Swahili buildings that transport one back to a bygone period. A fragrance of spices permeates the air, and the ancient tales reverberate through the walls.

Fort Jesus is a UNESCO World Heritage Site that offers a glimpse into the past. With its illustrious past as a Portuguese bastion, this impressive fortification provides expansive ocean vistas and an insight into the region's nautical history. The sea wind carries the echoes of maritime exploits and the tenacity of a coastal city that has withstood the test of time.

A seaside excursion wouldn't be complete without a visit to the sea. You can dunk your toes into the warm Indian Ocean embrace on Mombasa's white sand beaches. Beaches are places where people gather to unwind and have fun, whether by swimming, tanning, or just listening to the waves' soothing melody.

The perfume of beach food beckons as the day goes on. Offering a combination of Swahili, Arab, and Indian cuisines, Mombasa is a culinary pleasure. Taste the renowned Swahili biryani, revel in the succulent seafood from the coast, and let the spices take your palate on a gourmet voyage.

Throughout the afternoon, discover the fascinating aquatic life at Haller Park, a wildlife refuge that highlights the fragile balance between land and water. In this idyllic seaside setting, crocodiles, hippos, and giraffes live in peace and provide a unique viewpoint on conservation efforts.

The day ride from Nairobi to Mombasa becomes a treasure mine of memories as the sun sets and colors of pink and orange dance over the horizon. Traveling back under the starry African sky is a contemplative detour that enables you to bring the essence of the coast back to the center of Kenya.

PRACTICAL TIPS
Safety Precautions

Nairobi is a generally safe city, but it is important to know your surroundings and take precautions against crime. Here are some safety precautions to take in Nairobi:

- Steer clear of nighttime solo strolls, particularly in remote places. If you must go by yourself at night, remain in well-lit places and pay attention to your surroundings.
- When using public transportation, particularly matatus, use caution. Since matatus are notorious for being congested and dangerous, it's critical to be alert to your surroundings and take safety measures to keep yourself safe from pickpockets and other thieves.
- When taking food or beverages from strangers, use caution. It's crucial to be cautious while taking food and beverages from strangers since there have been cases of drugging and robbery.
- Use caution while flaunting pricey jewelry or gadgets. This may turn you into a target for thieves.
- Keep an eye on your surroundings and be ready to alert the authorities to any strange activities.

Here are some additional tips for staying safe in Nairobi:

- Make copies of your visa and passport, then store them somewhere secure. Keep a copy of your visa and passport with you always; keep the originals in a secure location.
- Sign up at the consulate or embassy of Kenya. They'll find it simpler to contact you in an emergency if they do this.
- Recognize Kenya's present state of politics and security. Steer clear of any known restless places.
- Obtain traveler's insurance. This will safeguard you in any unforeseen circumstances, such as medical crises or misplaced baggage.

By following these safety precautions, you can minimize your risk of becoming a victim of crime in Nairobi.

Here are some emergency contact numbers in Nairobi:

- Police: 999
- Ambulance: 999
- Fire department: 999
- Tourist hotline: +254 733 800 800

Health Information

Here is some important health information for travelers to Nairobi, Kenya:

- Immunizations: Before visiting Nairobi, ensure you are up to date on all your vaccines. Yellow fever, hepatitis A and B, typhoid, tetanus, diphtheria, cholera, measles, mumps, and rubella (MMR) are a few immunizations that are advised.
- Malaria: Since Nairobi is situated in a region where malaria is prevalent, it is crucial to take preventative measures. Using insect repellent, taking antimalarial medicine, and dressing in long sleeves and trousers at night are some suggested preventative methods against malaria.
- Waterborne infections: It's crucial to avoid raw fruits and vegetables in Nairobi and only drink bottled or boiling water.
- Sun protection: Since Nairobi lies close to the equator, wearing sun protection gear is essential. Wearing a hat, sunglasses, and sunscreen are a few suggested sun protection techniques.
- Medical care: There are many excellent clinics and hospitals in Nairobi. However, travel insurance is crucial in case you get ill while away from home.

Here is some additional health information for travelers to Nairobi:

- Altitude sickness: Given Nairobi's high altitude, it's critical to be mindful of the symptoms, which include headache, lightheadedness, and dyspnea. Relaxing and hydrating well is critical if you have any of these symptoms.
- Pollution: If you have asthma or other respiratory issues, you should be particularly mindful of the hazards associated with Nairobi's sometimes high levels of air pollution. Avoiding congested areas and wearing a mask outside are two advised safety measures.
- Food safety: When eating in Nairobi, it's crucial to exercise caution. Eat only prepared meals; stay away from fresh fruits and vegetables.

Useful Phrases

Greetings

- Jambo - Hello
- Habari? - How are you?
- Nzuri - Good
- Salama? - Are you well?
- Sawa - Fine

Politeness

- Asante - Thank you.

- Karibu - You're welcome.
- Tafadhali - Please
- Hapana - No
- Ndio - Yes
- Pole - Sorry
- Samahani - Excuse me.

Getting around

- Nipe tiketi ya kwenda (place) - Give me a ticket to (place)
- Hii basi/matatu inakwenda (place)? - Does this bus/matatu go to (place)?
- Kuna (place) karibu hapa? - Is there a (place) near here?
- Ni wapi ninaweza kupata (place)? - Where can I find a (place)?
- Ninaweza kupata taxi hapa? - Can I get a taxi here?

Shopping

- Ni shilingi ngapi? - How much is this?
- Napenda kununua (thing) - I would like to buy (thing)
- Unaweza kunipa punguzo? - Can I have a discount?
- Ni wapi posso kubadilisha pesa? - Where can I change money?
- Food and drink
- Nipe menyu - Give me the menu

- Napenda kuagiza (food or drink) - I would like to order (food or drink)
- Bili tafadhali - The bill, please

Other useful phrases

- Sijui - I don't know.
- Msaada! - Help!
- Ninazungumza Kiingereza kidogo - I speak a little English
- Poleni sana - I'm very sorry.
- Asante sana - Thank you very much.

SUSTAINABLE TOURISM
Eco-Friendly Practices

Nairobi is a rapidly growing city, and its residents are becoming increasingly aware of the importance of environmental sustainability. Here are some eco-friendly practices that are gaining popularity in Nairobi:

- Rainwater harvesting is the practice of gathering and holding onto rainwater for future use. Nairobi residents often engage in this activity as it may lessen the city's dependency on public water sources.
- Solar energy is still another well-liked environmentally beneficial method in Nairobi. Solar panels may be used to heat water or produce power.
- The process of turning organic waste into nutrient-rich soil is called composting. Nairobi residents often engage in this activity as it might lessen the quantity of rubbish in landfills.
- Recycling is the practice of repurposing garbage to create new items and materials. Nairobi residents often engage in this activity as it may help save natural resources and lessen the quantity of rubbish in landfills.
- Sustainable modes of transportation: In Nairobi, people are increasingly using walking, cycling, and public transit more

and more. These choices lessen both road congestion and air pollution.

Apart from these specific actions, the Kenyan government is also implementing measures to encourage environmental sustainability. To encourage the use of renewable energy, for instance, the government has started various programs. One such program is the Feed-in Tariff program, which offers cash rewards to people and companies that install renewable energy systems.

Nairobi is also making efforts to become a greener city. For instance, the Nairobi Green Building Code mandates that all new construction in the city adhere to strict environmental guidelines. This is just one of the many programs the city has implemented to support green building practices.

Nairobi residents are dedicated to creating a more environmentally friendly city. Nairobi is well on its path to becoming more sustainable by implementing eco-friendly practices and supporting governmental efforts.

Here are some additional eco-friendly practices that you can adopt while visiting Nairobi:

- Encourage neighborhood companies that are dedicated to sustainability. Many companies in Nairobi are making efforts to lessen their influence on the environment. Supporting these companies will enable the city to become more sustainable.

- Cut down on the amount of single-use plastics you use. In Kenya, single-use plastics represent a significant environmental issue. Bring your own shopping bags, cutlery, and water bottles to help reduce the amount of plastic you use.
- Consider how much water you use. In Kenya, water is a valuable resource. You may contribute to water conservation by taking shorter showers and shutting off the faucet when brushing your teeth.
- Honor the surrounding surroundings. Ensure no trace while visiting national parks and other natural places. This entails clearing up your waste and trying not to annoy the local animals.

Responsible Wildlife Tourism

Nairobi is a great city for wildlife tourism, as it is home to several national parks and game reserves. However, it is important to be responsible when engaging in wildlife tourism to minimize the impact on the animals and their environment. Here are some tips for responsible wildlife tourism in Nairobi:

- Select a trustworthy trip provider. Make sure you choose a trustworthy tour operator dedicated to responsible tourism when making a reservation for a wildlife trip. This implies that the tour operator ought to be well-versed in the ecology

and fauna of the area, and they should take precautions to minimize their influence.
- Show consideration for the animals. It's important to respect the animals and their surroundings while observing nature. This entails avoiding proximity, creating quiet, and disposing of trash.
- Encourage environmental initiatives. In Kenya, many conservation initiatives are in progress. You may contribute to preserving the wildlife and its environment by supporting these initiatives.

Here are some additional tips for responsible wildlife tourism in Nairobi:
- Do not go to wildlife reserves and national parks at the busiest times of the year. Peak season usually occurs in the dry months, when there is a greater concentration of animals around water sources. The animals may get overcrowded and more stressed as a result of this.
- Don't give the animals food. By changing their natural diet, feeding the animals may increase their reliance on humans. The animals may become aggressive as a result of it.
- Never remove trinkets from the wild. Bringing home trinkets from the outdoors may harm the ecosystem and exacerbate the dwindling numbers of animals.

- Notify the authorities of any poaching activities. In Kenya, poaching poses a major risk to animal populations. Be careful to notify the authorities immediately if you see any poaching activities.

Community Initiatives

Nairobi is a city with a vibrant and diverse community, and several community initiatives are underway to improve its residents' lives. Here are a few examples:

- Korogocho Community Development Initiative (KCDI) is a neighborhood-based group that strives to make the slum's inhabitants' lives better. KCDI provides various services and initiatives, including programs for economic empowerment, healthcare, and education.
- The Mathare Hope Community Centre (MHCC) is a community-driven organization dedicated to enhancing the quality of life for those who live in the Mathare slum. The MHCC provides various services and initiatives, such as healthcare, education, and job training.
- The multi-stakeholder Nairobi River Restoration Initiative (NRRI) aims to restore the Nairobi River. The NRRI has carried out a variety of initiatives to enhance the river's water quality and develop green areas along its banks.

- Nairobi Green City Initiative (NGCI): This multi-stakeholder project aims to improve Nairobi's sustainability and quality of life. To advance sustainable transportation, renewable energy, and green construction techniques, NGCI has put in place a variety of initiatives.
- Slum Dwellers International (SDI): Nairobi is home to several of the organization's worldwide network of slum dwellers. The mission of SDI is to enable slum dwellers to better their neighborhoods and lives.

These are just a few of the many community projects that Nairobi is now experiencing. These programs improve people's quality of life and make Nairobi a better place for all to live.

Nairobi is home to many unofficial community projects in addition to these official ones. To address particular problems in their communities, locals have organized a variety of self-help organizations, for instance. For instance, self-help organizations have been established to provide their members financial assistance, healthcare, and education.

Nairobi's residents are dedicated to improving their city for all. You may improve Nairobi's citizens' quality of life by contributing to community projects.

CONCLUSION

We would like to express our sincere appreciation for allowing our travel guide to be your companion as you travel through the colorful heart of East Africa as you approach the last pages of our Nairobi travel guide. Nairobi, a vibrant metropolis full of surprises around every corner, has revealed its mysteries to you, and we hope that this book has been a dependable travel companion.

We have journeyed through Nairobi's rich history in these pages, from its modest beginnings as a railway camp to its current position as a bustling city. We have experienced the captivating vistas of Nairobi National Park, interacted with the lively locals at the Maasai Market, and appreciated the special allure of the Giraffe Center. Nairobi has established itself as a location that skillfully combines the natural with the urban, offering outdoor activities and cultural encounters.

Nairobi is a remarkable travel destination because of its vibrant nightlife, diversified eating scene, and sustainable tourism efforts, all of which are covered in detail in our handbook. Travelers seeking animal encounters, cultural immersion, or mouthwatering cuisine will find Nairobi very accommodating, with a wide range of activities to suit all tastes.

Remember the sounds of the animals in the national park, the vivid colors of the Maasai Market, and the unforgettable experience of feeding a giraffe at the Giraffe Centre as you prepare to say goodbye to Nairobi. The people who walk the streets of Nairobi have a lasting impression on their spirits.

In addition to providing useful advice, we hope this tour has inspired you to explore more of Nairobi's core neighborhoods. Your adventure ends here, yet it becomes a collection of memories ready to be made.

We thank you once again for selecting our Nairobi travel guide. May the memories you make in Nairobi last long after you leave, and may your travels there be as limitless as the city's spirit.

Safe travels until we cross paths again on a different page of exploration.

Karibu Tena! (Welcome Again!)

Printed in Great Britain
by Amazon